OMG!

Enjoy!
Hollis

COOKBOOK

OH MY GOSH!
I'm in college, and I never learned to cook!

HOLLIS LEDBETTER

Tate Publishing & Enterprises

Published by Tate Publishing & Enterprises, LLC
127 E. Trade Center Terrace | Mustang, Oklahoma 73064 USA
1.888.361.9473 | www.tatepublishing.com

Tate Publishing is committed to excellence in the publishing industry. The company reflects the philosophy established by the founders, based on Psalm 68:11,
"The Lord gave the word and great was the company of those who published it."

Book design copyright © 2011 by Tate Publishing, LLC. All rights reserved.

Published in the United States of America

ISBN: 978-1-61663-959-4
1. Cooking; General
2. Cooking; Methods, Quick & Easy
11.04.04

In Dedication to Ann Haughton Sample

1921–2009

Mother, Mentor, and Friend

This book was a joyous gift to write. What made it most special was working with my best friend, my hero: my mother and artist, Ann Sample. Her beauty and talent sparkled inside and out and touched all those who knew her. She loved the whimsical, the unseen space between lines, and felt that no matter which way you looked at a painting, whether upside down or sideways, a person should always be able to "see a painting." Her whimsical art can be seen in illustrations sprinkled throughout the book, showing the typical angst of a student cooking for the first time. It was the expressions on the students' faces she drew that at times led me to create the title of a recipe. My mother always said: "When I'm creating, it assumes a mind of its own. Art usually takes an unforeseen turn. I have thought of my paintings as 'Art with a Twinkle.'"

A well-known artist, Ann studied at the Toledo Museum, owned a studio where she taught, and showed in numerous art shows throughout the years. Ann was always seen wearing a beautiful hat, with paintbrush in hand. Ann passed away just as the book was finished. I am so blessed to have been able to share this experience with her. Each night when the stars twinkle, I will always see her magic. I have been so blessed. Mom told me that she did these drawings as a gift to me, but I want to thank her for sharing her art with you, dear reader; she was my dear friend and this kind act will always be an inspiration for me.

It is my intent to use some of the proceeds of this book to fund:

The Ann Haughton Sample Foundation

The foundation's purpose is twofold: to provide children, who otherwise would not, with the opportunity to go to art camp so they may be touched by art; and to further expose the world to my mother's beautiful work.

Acknowledgements

Many people have contributed to the joy of creating this book. It has been a fun and creative way to learn, prepare, and experience cooking. I say a special thank you to each of you who have added to the suggestions and editing you have given.

A very special thank you to Bill Ledbetter, Cayden Jordan, and Lucy Harris. Lucy provided invaluable support for a new author. Another thank you goes to my amazing daughter, Cayden. Her writing and editing skills added so many ideas to this book. A special thank you to my loving husband, Bill, who endlessly organized and edited.

And to the rest of my children: Oakley, Marlyn, and Jakob who were experimental with reading and re-reading my ideas and recipes over and over and for adding many of their proven recipes.

To all of my friends who gave me their family home recipes for me to use, I say thank you.

And my hero, my mother, Ann Sample, whose talented drawings are generously sprinkled throughout the book, showing the typical teenage angst of a student cooking for the first time. It was the expressions she drew that many times created the title of a recipe and the thought that one would be thinking cooking for the first time.

Table of Contents

Foreword

Although it seems like it was just yesterday, over thirty years ago, Hollis opened the door of her Atlanta home and I first encountered the magnetic smile and infectious giggle for which she is famous among her many friends. Then, as now, family togetherness and an exuberant celebration of life came together in the Ledbetter's kitchen to provide the aromatic focal point of their buoyant communication, which are both wholesome and entertaining, qualities which are reflected in the recipes of *OMG Cookbook; Oh My Gosh! I'm In College, and I Never Learned to Cook*! I am happy to say I have been blessed to be the beneficiary of enough of Hollis's cooking extravaganzas to recognize the eager anticipation I have when I know she is involved, my mind wondering what she'll come up with "this time" to surprise and delight. Like this enticing cookbook, Hollis is a party waiting for a place to happen; be it on a picnic blanket, around the coffee table in the den, or at an elegant formal dinner, she welcomes any opportunity to nourish the body and connect the spirit.

Several years ago my son, Noah, and one of the Ledbetter's daughters, "Cakie" (Cayden), were attending UGA, and we all had firsthand experience with concern for the culinary experiences of the college student. This book is more than an excellent cookbook and nutrition reference; rather, it has become an ICONic labor of life and love. With as many stops and starts as a growing family, it has grown to include the total range of ingredients from spicy, hilarious outbursts to soothing moments of quiet contemplation. It has been a long time coming, kind of like a well-planned and executed Thanksgiving dinner. *OMG* is a feast for the body, heart, mind, and spirit, which I heartily recommend for college students and first time cooks. However, it is also for anyone, like me, who wishes to build a happy life within the well-stocked kitchen, recognizing that home is where the heart is. And whether it is squeezed into a tiny apartment, snuggled up in a cabin on a creek, or grandly equipped in a traditional dream house, the heart of the home is a table like the one at the Ledbetter's, which satisfies the hungry appetite as it warms the soul with blessed good humor, a willing sense of adventure, and the comfort of cozy welcome.

—Lucy Harris
Co-author of *Simply American:
A Gentle Warrior & His People*

Registration

Start at the Beginning

What? We get to shop?

Core Classes:

Shopping List

Aluminum foil

Baking Pan

Blender

Can opener/bottle opener

Colander: This is for draining pasta and cleaning fruit and vegetables.

Crock-Pot: This makes life easier on those long days in a classroom.

Dish drainer and rack

Folding stainless steel steamer basket: Used for steaming vegetables to keep nutrients, texture, and color intact.

Garlic press

Large smooth blade knife: Use this knife for carving and chopping.

Meat thermometer

Muffin pan – small or large

One 11"x13" casserole dish

One cookie sheet

One frying pan

One large spoon

One six-quart pot

One eight-quart pot

One small saucepan

Plates, forks, knives, spoons, glasses: A set of four is needed.

Small paring knife: This knife is handy for cutting vegetables and fruits.

Spatula

Spice rack: Filled with the spices mentioned below in Basic Items to Have on Hand.

Strainer: Preferably, choose a stainless steel, tight-wire mesh, handheld version, which can also be used as a sifter.

Two candles: See PhD: Perfectly Hosted Dinners

Two cutting boards: Buy one wooden cutting board for vegetables and fruit and one plastic cutting board for beef, pork, poultry, and fish.

Two mixing bowls

Two pot holders: One for each hand or one for someone else's hand.

Notes:

Basic Items to Have on Hand

Shopping Tips:

Baking items: eggs, sugar, honey, baking soda, baking powder, flour, and vanilla

Bay Leaves: Be sure to remove from food before serving.

Boxed low-sodium broths: chicken, beef, and vegetable

Canned tomatoes: diced, whole, Italian style, sauce and paste

Canola oil

Cooking spray

OMG! She calls this "basic"?

Garlic powder

Garlic: Buy minced garlic bulbs in a jar. Refrigerate after opening.

Italian seasoning blend: Takes care of buying parsley, oregano, and rosemary.

Olive oil

Pasta: whole wheat or semolina; elbow, spaghetti, fettuccine, or any size and shape you prefer.

Pepper

Rice: long grain, whole wheat and white rice. Use white rice for "fried rice."

Salt: Preferably sea salt

Sauces: marinara and pasta

Soy sauce

Worcestershire sauce

- Use cloth bags when going to the grocery store.

- Recycle and use plastic containers with lids for storage. This will help reduce trash in the environment.

- Discuss with your other roommates, before moving in, which supplies they plan to bring. This prevents the repeat of items, such as too many forks and not enough knives, etc.

 Parents, siblings, aunts and uncles, and grandparents: All of the items listed are great graduation gifts to help your student be successful on their own in their first kitchen.

Terms

Sift: Sometimes a recipe will call for sifting. This is when you add the other dry ingredients into the flour. If you don't have a sifter, substitute a stainless steel, tight, mesh colander. Put the dry ingredients into the colander, and place the colander over a bowl. Using a fork, press back and forth on the dry ingredients until all ingredients fall through the mesh into the bowl.

Mince: This means to cut vegetables into teeny tiny pieces.

Cube: Cut meat or vegetables into small square chunks; not as small as minced.

Chop: Cut your vegetables into small, uniform pieces. Cutting food about the same size helps ensure that all the food is evenly cooked through and done at the same time.

Sauté: To cook in a shallow pan using a small amount of hot oil while keeping the food moving. If you are sautéing garlic and onions, put a small amount of oil in a skillet. Let the oil get hot, but watch it to make sure the oil does not burn. When the oil is hot, it will shimmer. Add garlic and onions and turn the heat down to medium-low. Sauté in the oil until the onions are translucent—until they look clear. Keep heat regulated so there is no "smoking."

Science Lab: Measuring and Equivalents

Abbreviations

t. = teaspoon

T. = tablespoon

C. = cup

pt. = pint

qt. = quart

oz. = ounce

lb. = pound

Do I need to memorize all this?

Equivalents

1 C. =16 T.

2 C. liquid =1 pt.

4 C. liquid =1 qt.

1 oz. = 2 T.

16 oz. =1 lb.

2 pt. =1 qt.

4 qt. liquid = 1 gallon

1 liter = approx. 4 C. or 1 qt.

8 oz. =1 C.

3 t. =1T.

It's okay to double or triple a recipe, but more than that gets tricky…better make two double batches.

What to Look for When Buying Fish

- First and foremost, pay attention to the smell. You will know fish is bad if it has a strong "fishy" smell.

- The eyes of the fish should be clear, not dull, and certainly not sunken in.

- Cuts of fish that are browning or yellow around the edges are suspect.

- If you purchase frozen, always make sure it has been securely wrapped to prevent freezer burn. When thawing fish, it is best to thaw it overnight in the refrigerator. Do not open the package until you are ready to prepare the fish for cooking.

For thicker cuts of fish like salmon or grouper steaks, you may like to grill or broil. Thinner cuts may be lightly breaded and pan-fried. Experiment with different ways of cooking fish. Be aware that some fish may contain higher levels of mercury and should be eaten sparingly.

Who says you can't be the biggest fish in the pond?

 Fish is low in fat and has lots of protein. Salmon is full of Omega-3s, which are very good for you because they are a good source of antioxidant compounds.

Sponges and Dish Towels

Always wash dish towels in the washing machine in hot water. Sponges can be washed in the dishwasher, or they can be put in the microwave for sixty seconds. This helps kill bacteria. Always use a clean dish towel when drying dishes to prevent the spread of bacteria, or use a dish drainer to air dry.

Cutting Boards

It is always best to use *two separate* cutting boards when preparing a meal. Use a wooden cutting board for your vegetables and a plastic one for beef, pork, poultry, and fish. You can sanitize a wooden cutting board by washing it with hot, soapy water; letting it dry; and rubbing with oil after each use. When wooden cutting boards become old and cracked, it is best if you dispose of them so bacteria does not grow.

 Remember these tips: Better safe than sorry!

Please tell me I used the right cutting board! Pleeeeease!

Special Care for Preparin', Cookin', and Storin'

Toss foods that show the slightest sign of spoilage. Watch for bulges on cans, bugs in dry goods, and any changes in the smell or appearance that may indicate spoilage.

Check bread for unusual colors (mold) before you eat. Storage in refrigerator will slow the process of mold growth, but will not stop it. When one piece of bread starts to mold, don't taste another. Molds don't need light, and they thrive on gases, which will contaminate the other pieces.

Beef, pork, poultry, and fish spoil more quickly than fruits or vegetables. It is important they be handled carefully. When buying, look for packages that are tightly wrapped and cold. Put all beef, pork, poultry, fish, and cold dairy products (such as cheese, butter, and milk) in the refrigerator immediately. When ready to prepare, defrost frozen beef, pork, poultry, and fish in the refrigerator, not at room temperature. Make sure no meat juices drip on any other food. Isolate by putting in a freezer zipper bag, and then put the whole thing in a bowl large enough to contain any drips.

Safe storage is very important. Keep your refrigerator set at thirty-eight to forty degrees Fahrenheit. Cook within several days of purchase, or freeze right away. If you've cooked meat or poultry, better use it or lose it! Cook fresh fish the day you buy it or at least by the next day.

Raw, frozen meat should be kept no longer than four to six months. Uncooked poultry can be frozen for six to nine months, and cooked poultry can be kept four to six months. Uncooked fish that is fatter, such as salmon, can be frozen for two to three months; leaner cuts can be frozen up to six months. Cooked fish can be frozen for four to six months. All food must be wrapped *airtight* or it will get "freezer-burned" in the freezer. Throw away any freezer-burned food.

Clean It!

Keep it clean, and that means everything: hands, utensils, cutting boards, counters, and sinks. Remember: always wash hands after handling anything *raw*! Don't put cooked food on the same plate that you had raw foods on, or you may lose it in more ways than one.

Cook and Look!

Cooking meat kills nasty bacteria. Cooked pork should not be pink, and the juices should run clear and register 165-degree internal temperature. Be fair to both sides when broiling, grilling, or cooking on the stove. Flip the meat at least once. Some types of fish are the exception. The best way to test for proper temperature is with a meat thermometer, which is very inexpensive and can be purchased at your grocery store. Reheat leftovers at 165 degrees or until hot and steamy throughout. You can also reheat in the microwave. If it looks bad, throw it away. If it smells bad, throw it away. If you think it's too old, throw it away. If in doubt, throw it away.

Don't Skip Class: Tips and Substitutions

Tips on Fat:

Mayonnaise or dressings: Use 1 t. of mayonnaise, and mix with 2 t. of reduced fat sour cream, for making egg or tuna salad, producing a lower fat content salad.
Canned fish: Use water-packed canned products instead of oil-packed.
Fat cuts of meat: Use leaner cuts of meat or ground meat marked "lean."
Skin on chicken: Remove skin before cooking. Skin on is cheaper than skinned chicken, but you don't have to eat the skin if you're looking to reduce the fat!

Tips on Sodium (Salt):

Learning early to reduce salt intake is important because it is one of the leading causes of high blood pressure and places us at risk for heart attack and stroke as we age. Omit salt or reduce salt by half in most recipes. Cook foods without adding salt. Don't put the salt shaker on the table. Try and use sea salt or a brand of non-salt. Non-salt will give you the same flavor; with sea salt you will realize you won't need to use as much as you would like to with regular salt.

Seasoning salt or spice mixes with salt: Use salt-free seasoning and spice mixes. Use herbs, spices, lemon juice, or vinegar to flavor food instead of salt. Be cautious with seasonings high in sodium, which include catsup, chili sauce, chili powder, bouillon cubes, barbecue sauce, soy sauce, Worcestershire sauce, and meat tenderizers. It is fun to learn and experiment with various herbs to spice foods, and your friends will be so impressed that you really know how to cook. You may impress them so much they will want to learn how to cook this way.

Frozen or canned vegetables: Choose frozen vegetables without sauces, and use no salt added if eating canned goods. Rinsing canned vegetables will help reduce sodium.

Sugar Tips:

Reduce sugar by 1/4 to 1/3 in baked goods and desserts. If a recipe calls for 1 C. of sugar, use 3/4 C. and add 1 to 2 t. of cinnamon, or 1 t. vanilla, or ¼ t. almond extract, which will give the impression of sweetness. Replacing sugar with amounts of Splenda* works well for most baked products. Experiment with syrup or pureed fruit, such as no-sugar added applesauce or sugar-free syrup. Try it, you may like it!

*Use of brand names is not an endorsement of the product, rather a reference to brands that have such widespread use that the product is known by its brand name.

Ways to Increase Fiber:
The Things We Know Now That We Didn't Know Then

Replace white rice with whole grain, brown rice, or whole-wheat couscous.

All-purpose flour: Substitute unbleached whole-wheat flour for up to 1/2 of the all-purpose flour. For example, if a recipe calls for 2 C. flour, try 1 C. all-purpose flour and 1 C. minus 1 T. unbleached whole wheat flour.

White Bread: Use 100 percent whole wheat bread or 100 percent whole grain bread, both made with unbleached flour. Whole wheat and whole grain bread provides more fiber to your diet.

Iceberg lettuce: For increased nutrition, use romaine lettuce, endive, and other leafy lettuces or baby spinach. For sandwiches, use broccoli sprouts. They are full of vitamins and add flavor to a sandwich. Basil leaves also enhance the taste of any sandwich.

ICONs: What Clicks!

 Reminders of safety and cooking suggestions.

 The Kitty Reminder

Don't forget to feed the kitty: Place a jar or any container in one area of the kitchen, and each roommate will put a dollar or pocket change in each day. This is known as a "kitty." A dollar a day multiplied by four roommates over thirty days equals $120 a month. Taking turns, each roommate will, when it is his or her time to shop, take the money that is in the kitty to buy common supplies such as dishwasher soap, paper towels, laundry detergent, etc.

Roommates will most likely want to buy their own food to cook. Having a kitty makes it easier to share in buying the common supplies. Sharing the cost of common supplies that all roommates use really helps "getting along." The kitty keeps one person from feeling he or she is carrying more weight or expense.

Who's the new kitty around here?

The Three Bs:
Boiling, Broiling, and Baking

I was supposed to bake it?

If they stick, the masterpiece is done; but if they fall, you'd better run.

Cooking Pasta

Noodle art is in the air.
Where they land we do not care.
Ceiling art is lots of fun.
And you can tell when they are done.

Pasta absorbs a lot of water, so use a *big* pot. Fill pot ¾ full with water, and add 1 T. olive oil. Bring the water to a rolling boil before putting the pasta in the water. When water is at a "rolling boil" it is boiling vigorously and cannot be stopped by stirring. Add one package of pasta, and stir until it is all submerged. Stay with your pasta. Overcooking is easy to do. Stir every two minutes to keep the pasta from sticking together. The best way to test if the pasta is done is by tasting it. If the texture is *soft and firm, or "al dente,"* then it is done. It should be semi-soft, but not mushy. There should be a slight springiness when you bite on the pasta. Drain and shake the cooked pasta in a colander. Be sure all of the water is drained. Do not rinse the pasta. Return the pasta to the dry pot. Stir in an additional 1 T. olive oil and toss together, which will lubricate the pasta and keep it from sticking.

Notes:

Homemade Egg Salad

Ingredients:

6 hardboiled eggs

2 T. mayonnaise

1 T. sweet relish

1/2 t. mustard (optional)

dash of paprika

salt and pepper to taste

A watched pot never boils!

Directions:

Bring a pot of water to a boil (enough water to cover eggs). Boil eggs for nine minutes. Drain water, and put eggs in ice water. Let the eggs sit for six minutes. Peel and discard the shells. Chop eggs in a bowl. Add all the ingredients and mix together. Salt and pepper to taste. Top with paprika.

Serve on whole grain bread with lettuce and tomato.

 To lower the fat content in this recipe, use 1 T. of reduced fat sour cream with 1 T. regular mayonnaise.

The Oriental Noodle

Ingredients:

½ head broccoli, cut into small pieces

2 large green peppers, diced

1 carrot, diced

1 handful snow peas

1 bunch spinach, thoroughly cleaned

1 package of rice noodles

4 garlic cloves, divided and crushed

½ jar oriental sauce

4 T. olive or canola oil, devided

4 T. butter

1 loaf of French bread

Snow peas?

Directions:

Fill a large pot with water. Drop in 1 T. of olive oil. Bring to a rolling boil. Put pasta in the water in small bunches so the water doesn't stop boiling. Stir every two minutes to keep pasta from sticking together. Cook according to the instructions on the package. When pasta is cooked, drain in a colander; don't rinse. Put back in pot and toss with 1 T. olive oil. While cooking the pasta, prepare the vegetables. Cut the stem off of the snow pea pods. Remove the string on the edge of the pods by pulling down.

In a large pan, add 2 T. of olive oil or canola oil. Sauté ½ of crushed garlic clove. When garlic is light brown, remove from pan. Add carrots, broccoli, and green pepper

*Continued on next page

to the pan; sauté until slightly tender. Add snow peas and spinach; sauté two minutes. Put all ingredients together with pasta and toss with ½ jar of the oriental sauce.

While pasta is cooking, slit the French bread lengthwise. In a small saucepan melt the butter with the rest of the garlic; then pour the melted butter in the slit. Wrap the bread in aluminum foil, and bake at 350 degrees for twenty minutes until heated through and "crusty."

 Do not rinse the pasta when cooked, because it removes the starch from the noodles. Just add a little olive oil and mix or toss until coated.

Notes:

Spinach, Noodles, and Cheese

Ingredients:

- 1 loaf of French bread
- 1 garlic clove, crushed
- 4 T. butter
- 1 package fresh spinach, thoroughly washed
- 4 ripe tomatoes cut into wedges
- 2 T. olive oil
- 1 package of angel hair or spaghetti noodles
- 1 package of feta cheese

I wonder if I'll get my deposit back?

Directions:

In a saucepan melt ½ stick of butter and one crushed clove of garlic. Slice a loaf of French bread down the middle, and spread the butter mixture inside the bread. Wrap in aluminum foil and bake at 350 degrees for twenty minutes.

While the bread is cooking, bring an 8 qt. pot of water with 1 T. olive oil to a boil. Put in one package of angel hair or spaghetti noodles, and cook according to the instructions on package. While the noodles are cooking, add 1" of water to another pot, and insert your steamer basket so that the water level is under the bottom of steamer. Bring water to a gentle boil. Put spinach in first; then add tomato wedges and crumbled feta on top in the steamer. Cook until feta has softened over the spinach. Be sure the steam can get through the spinach so all ingredients cook at the same time. Place the spinach, tomatoes, and feta on top of individual bowls of noodles.

When using fresh spinach, be sure to run it under water for several cycles to insure that all grit is removed.

Who Cares If You Doodle Your Noodle

Ingredients:

2½ T. olive oil

1 fresh garlic clove, crushed

½ package angel hair pasta

¼ C. Parmesan cheese

1 loaf French bread

Directions:

Fill an 8 qt. pot with water. Place on high heat, and bring it to a rolling boil. Put in pasta, and stir every two minutes to keep pasta from sticking together. Cook according to the directions on the package. Heat 1 ½ T. olive oil in a large pan and sauté crushed garlic clove until slightly brown. Toss the pasta with the olive oil and garlic, and top with Parmesan cheese. Serve with toasted French bread and one of the salads found in The Dreaded Freshman Fifteen.

How do you doodle a noodle in numerous ways?

Tuna Melts on Rye Toast

Ingredients:

- 1 can white tuna, in water
- 1 celery stalk, chopped fine
- 1 T. mayonnaise
- 1 T. pickle relish
- 1 slice rye bread
- salt and pepper to taste
- 1 slice of Swiss or provolone cheese

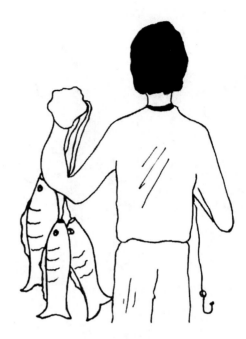

Clean? They look clean to me!

Directions:

Drain water from tuna. Mix all the ingredients together, except the bread and cheese. Toast one piece of rye bread. Put a scoop of tuna on the bread, and top with provolone or Swiss cheese. To make an open face *melt* sandwich, put the sandwich on a cookie sheet and place under the broiler until cheese melts and starts to brown. Keep your eye on this so it does not burn.

Notes:

They'll never miss the extra bacon!

Notes:

Broiling 101

B.B.S.T.: Basil, Bacon, Spinach, and Tomato Melt

Ingredients:

whole-grain or rye bread (1 piece per sandwich)

2 slices cooked bacon for each sandwich

1 tomato slice, per sandwich

1 pkg. leaf spinach

2 basil leaves washed and dried, per sandwich

1 t. reduced fat mayonnaise for each piece of bread

1 slice of low fat Swiss or reduced fat mozzarella cheese per sandwich

Directions:

Depending on how many people are eating, take out enough bread. Put 1 t. of reduced fat mayo on each piece of bread. Layer the tomato, spinach, bacon, and basil. Top with cheese. Place the sandwich in your oven broiler and cook until cheese bubbles and turns slightly brown. Keep a close eye on the melt so that the cheese doesn't burn.

This sandwich can be made with any of your favorite deli meats. Just follow the same directions, and add your meat. You could leave out the bacon.

Lemon Salmon

Ingredients:

2 small pieces salmon

3 T. olive oil

1 T. Worcestershire sauce

1 lemon, juiced

½ T. lemon zest (optional)

salt and pepper to taste

I'm famished. Would you like fish tonight?

Directions:

Set rack three inches from the top of the broiler. Wash fish and pat dry with a towel. Remove skin and any bones you see. To make the marinade: mix the olive oil and lemon juice in a bowl. Add salt, pepper, and Worcestershire sauce. You may want to grate the lemon skin, and then add it to the marinade. To make lemon zest, use a grater and push the lemon back and forth over the grater. Put fillets in the bowl, and marinate the fish for twenty minutes. If you don't have time to marinate, just rub the fish front and back with marinade and put in a shallow casserole dish. Put the fish in the broiler and broil for five to seven minutes or until done. While cooking, do not turn the fish over. Baste while cooking every three minutes using the remainder of the marinade.

*To test when the fish is done, stick a fork into the fish. When you pull it apart, it should flake off and easily separate. If it still looks fleshy pink, cook a minute or two longer. Remember, when you eat, there are **always** bones in fish!*

Baking 101

Cover Me Up: Easy Chicken

"They are so impressed!"

"I know!"

Ingredients:

2 skinless chicken breasts

1 can cream of celery soup

1 can of water

1 lemon cut in half

¼ C. Parmesan cheese

Directions:

In a pot on the stove, heat the celery soup with one can of water on medium heat. Add the lemon juice to the soup by squeezing the lemon juice through your fingers to catch the seeds. Place the chicken in a greased casserole dish and pour the soup mixture evenly over the chicken. Top with Parmesan cheese. Bake at 350 degrees for approximately forty-five minutes.

If you are feeding more than just yourself, buy additional chicken. Legs and thighs are less expensive than breast meat and will taste just as delicious in this simple recipe. If you cook a whole chicken, boil it in a large pot for forty-five minutes. Let it cool, and then pull the meat off of the bones. Place the chicken pieces in a casserole dish, double the rest of the ingredients, and follow the recipe. If using the boiled chicken, which will be cooked, you will need to cook the casserole in the oven for only twenty five minutes. Just make sure it is heated all the way through.

When you cut into the chicken, the juices should run clear. If you see red or pink, cook some more. Always wash your hands after handling raw chicken!

Sweeeet Acorn Squash

Ingredients:

- 1 medium acorn squash
- 2 t. butter
- 2 t. dark brown sugar or honey

I made it myself!

Directions:

Cut acorn squash into two halves, and scrape out the seeds. In a casserole dish, put each half flat down with skin side up. Add a small amount of water enough to cover the bottom. Bake at 350 degrees for forty minutes or until you can poke a fork easily through the skin. When cooked, turn the squash over and put in 1 t. of butter and 1 t. brown sugar or honey in each squash. Mix the squash, butter, and sugar together with a fork.

 This goes great with an entrée such as pork chops, chicken, or fish.

Notes:

Cheesy Chicken Quesadilla

Ingredients:

4 flour tortillas, 6" round

4 chicken thighs, cooked and shredded

1 green bell pepper, sliced into thin slices

1 small onion, sliced into thin slices

2 C. mushrooms, sliced

4 T. shredded "Mexican" cheese

2 T. olive oil

This reminds me of my home!

Directions:

Bring a pot of water to a boil. Salt and pepper the chicken thighs, and put them in the boiling water. Boil for thirty minutes or until the chicken falls off the bone. Remove chicken, let cool, shred into pieces, and set aside. In a skillet put 1 T. of olive oil in a saucepan over medium heat. Add the sliced onions and green peppers, and cook in the skillet until the onions look translucent (clear). Add the mushrooms, and cook until tender. Divide the vegetables and shredded chicken mixture equally on two tortillas. Sprinkle the cheese evenly on the vegetable and chicken mixture. Place the remaining tortillas on top. Put 1 T. olive oil in a skillet and place over medium heat. Put the two filled tortillas into the heated skillet. Place a heavy, small ovenproof pan on top of the tortillas in the skillet. Cook for three minutes, flip, and cook an additional three minutes or until cheese has melted. Cut each quesadilla into four wedges. Makes two quesadillas or eight divided wedges. If you want more, repeat.

This is delicious served with guacamole and sour cream: See Guacamole recipe next page.

39

Side

Guacamole

Ingredients:

1 ripe avocado

1 lemon, juiced

1 garlic clove, crushed

1 dash of hot sauce

salt and pepper to taste

Directions:

Cut avocado in two pieces, cutting around the seed. Remove and discard the seed. Scoop out the pulp. Smash with a fork, and mix all ingredients together.

Notes:

The Dreaded Freshman Fifteen: Healthy Ways to Eat without Getting a Bigger Seat!

You may love fast food. It's easy to get, tastes good, and is easy to clean up. But fast food is fat food, and worst of all, it leads to the dreaded "freshman fifteen" weight gain!

This chapter is full of easy and economical recipes, offering alternative choices in eating. You will learn how to buy and cook in a healthy but delicious way.

Get the Skinny on Portion Control

Learn To See It, Not Overeat It

Grains

One slice = 1 serving of bread
A compact disc = 1 pancake
Half of baseball = 1/2 C. cooked rice, pasta
Size of a fist = 1 C. of cereal flakes
Hockey puck = 1/2 bagel

Fruits and Veggies

A baseball = 1 C. salad greens
A baseball = 1 medium fruit
A large egg = 1/2 C. raisins
A fist = 1 C. or 8 oz. salad greens
A fist = 1 serving of potato

Exercise controls your "portion" too!

Dairy and Cheese

Four stacked dice = 1 1/2 oz. cheese
Half of baseball = 1/2 C. ice cream
Size of a fist = 1 C. serving of milk, yogurt, or fresh greens
A thumb = 1 oz. of cheese
The tip of your thumb = 1 t. butter

Meats and Alternatives

Deck of cards = 3 oz. Meat, fish, poultry
Checkbook = 3 oz. grilled/baked fish
The palm of your hand = 3 oz. of meat

Fats

Canola and olive oil are most recommended:
A size equal to the tip of your thumb = 1 t. of oil
A thumb = 1 oz. of nuts
One ping pong ball = 2 T. peanut butter
Two handfuls = 1 oz. chips

Notes:

Why College Students Need This Cookbook!

This is the first recipe that my daughter, who graduated from the University of Georgia, cooked. When asked why she cooked this recipe, she said, "Because I didn't know how to cook!" This is the reason this cookbook was created. This is an easy beginner's recipe to help get you familiar with some basics.

Ingredients:

4 boneless chicken tenders

2 C. fresh or frozen spinach

½ C. cottage cheese

2 T. olive oil or canola oil

Your favorite chunky spaghetti sauce

Directions:

Heat 2 T. olive oil or canola oil in a large, flat frying pan. When oil is hot, add the chicken tenders. Lower the heat to medium and continue to cook for three minutes on the first side; turn the tenders over and cook an additional three minutes. Put a steamer basket in a pot. Add enough water to touch the bottom of the steamer basket. Put spinach in and cook until it looks wilted. Fresh spinach will wilt in four minutes or less. If you are using frozen spinach, follow the directions on the package. Drain and put spinach on plate; top with chicken tenders. Heat sauce and pour over chicken. Serve with cottage cheese.

Should I make this again? It's the only thing I know how to cook!

To test if the chicken is done, cut into one piece. The inside should be white and the juice clear. If you see any pink, cook some more! You may prefer to buy a bag of washed spinach so that you can make salads throughout the week with leftover spinach. If the spinach is already washed, it should not need to be washed again.

Notes:

Toss It Up Salads

I wonder what color I should make the dressing?

Garden Salad

Ingredients:

1 small head of fresh lettuce

1 small tomato

¼ C. scallions, chopped

¼ C. carrots, shredded

¼ C. cucumbers, diced

¼ C. croutons

Directions:

Wash and dry lettuce and tear into small bite size pieces. Cut tomato into four wedges. Mix all ingredients together. Toss with your favorite dressing.

Notes:

46

Make it Greek

Ingredients:

2 C. of romaine lettuce, tear into pieces

5 black kalamata olives

1 C. red onion

2 pepperoncini peppers thinly sliced

¼ C. feta cheese

1 bottle Greek dressing

Directions:

Prepare lettuce. Cut onion into thin strips. Mix first three ingredients together, except cheese. Crumble the feta cheese over the lettuce and add the pepperoncini, which can be found in the deli department. Pour 1 or 2 t. of Greek dressing. Mix well.

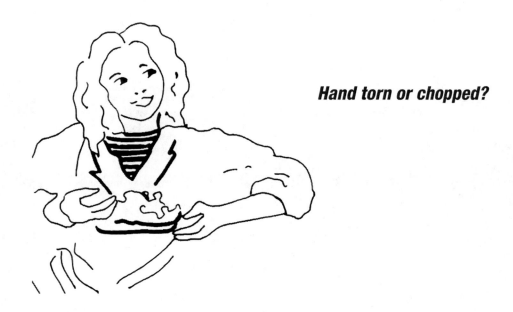

Hand torn or chopped?

Marlyn's Favorite Salad

Ingredients:

- 2 C. of romaine lettuce
- ½ C. goat cheese, crumbled
- 2 t. pine nuts
- 1 t. vinaigrette dressing
- 1 t. ranch dressing

Directions:

Tear lettuce into small pieces. Mix all ingredients together, except cheese. Mix vinaigrette and ranch together. Toss salad with dressing. Crumble cheese on top.

Notes:

Bill's Wedge

Ingredients:

   1 head of iceberg lettuce

   4 T. blue cheese dressing or your favorite dressing

   4 slices cooked bacon (Use bacon without nitrates, if available.)

Directions:

Cut the lettuce into four wedges. Pour 1 T. of dressing over each wedge. Crumble one slice of bacon over each wedge.

 Instead of using 4 T. of dressing, lower the fat by using 2 T. of your preferred dressing mixed with 2 T. of red wine vinegar.

Notes:

Stuff It!

Ingredients:

5 stalks of celery

5 T. pimento cheese mixture

5 pitted green olives, sliced thin

Directions:

To vein celery, snap the top leaves and pull down to remove the strings. Spread 1 T. pimento cheese on each celery stalk. Top with sliced green olives.

Celery makes me so happy!

 Celery can be stuffed with tuna or chicken salad, even peanut butter.

Notes:

Head Lettuce Salad

Ingredients:

1 head of iceberg lettuce

5 slices of cooked bacon, crumbled

1 C. tomatoes, diced

2 hard boiled eggs, diced

2 t. of you favorite salad dressing

Directions:

Pull off the outside lettuce leaves, discard, and thoroughly wash the lettuce head. Cut the lettuce into four wedge pieces. Evenly divide the bacon, tomatoes, and eggs for the four wedges. Sprinkle the crumbled bacon and diced tomatoes over each wedge of the iceberg lettuce. Top with the diced eggs and pour the salad dressing mixture on top. For a great taste, heat 2 t. of poppyseed dressing in the microwave for five seconds or until hot.

 To boil eggs, put the eggs in salted boiling water. Boil for nine minutes. Take the eggs out and put the eggs in a bowl with ice and water for six minutes. Make sure the eggs are covered with the ice water. This method makes them easy to peel.

Notes:

Mike's Favorite Chicken Salad

Ingredients:

2 C. chicken, diced (2 chicken breasts and 2 thighs)

½ package noodle shells

½ C. scallions, diced

½ C. celery, chopped into small bites

½ C. apple, chopped into small bites

½ C. grapes, diced

½ C. walnuts, chopped

2 t. curry

salt and pepper to taste

5 T. low fat mayonnaise

Directions:

In a large pot filled with water, cook the chicken for thirty-five minutes. The chicken should fall off the bone using a fork. When pricked, the juices should run clear. If pink, cook some more. Cool and cut into chunks. In a separate pot, cook noodles according to the directions on the package. Drain and cool to room temperature. Combine celery, apple, grapes, walnuts, scallions, noodles, and chicken. Add mayonnaise, curry, salt, and pepper to taste. Mix well. Serve on bib lettuce leaves. You can also stuff one large scoop in a wheat pita pocket.

 You can use 3 T. mayonnaise mixed with 2 T. low fat sour cream as a lower fat substitute. Or add a little mustard, just to give it an extra bite of flavor while reducing fat!

What's this "Freshman fifteen"?

Notes:

Lucy's Cucumber Salad

Ingredients:

1 t. dill, chopped if fresh

1 t. garlic powder

¼ C. water

1 t. canola oil

1 t. vinegar

1 T. sugar

½ t. pepper

½ red onion, diced

1 red bell pepper

3 cucumbers

Directions:

In a jar with a lid, pour in the water; add the oil and vinegar. Shake vigorously until well combined. Combine pepper, garlic powder, and sugar in a large bowl. Add the oil mixture to the garlic powder, pepper, sugar and mix well. Cut top and bottom off of red bell pepper. Cut down one side and unroll. Remove all seeds and white pulp, and cut in to ¼" slices. Peel and cut cucumbers in half lengthwise. Remove and discard seeds using the tip of spoon. Slice cucumbers in to ¼ " slices. Add bell pepper, onion, and cucumbers to the bowl. Stir until vegetables are well coated. Cover with plastic wrap and put in the refrigerator until cold throughout. It is best to refrigerate overnight or all day while you are in class. Sprinkle with dill before serving.

Nana's recipe has got to be on the Internet somewhere...

Notes:

Spinach Salad

Ingredients:

1 bunch fresh spinach leaves

½ C. button mushrooms, sliced

2 slices cooked bacon, crumbled

2 hard-boiled eggs

¼ C. low fat poppy seed dressing

1 T. butter

1 garlic clove, minced

2 slices bread

Directions:

Wash spinach leaves thoroughly; you can buy already washed spinach. Put spinach leaves on four individual plates. Peel the eggs and dice. Top spinach leaves with bacon, mushrooms, and eggs. In a saucepan over low heat, put in the poppy seed dressing, and heat. Drizzle 2 t. of the low fat poppy seed dressing over the salad. Melt 1 T. of butter and 1 clove of garlic in a saucepan. Rub this mixture on one side of a piece of your favorite bread. (Whole grain, sunflower, or rye would be best.) Cook under the broiler in your stove until slightly brown. (Keep a close eye on this! It can burn quickly.) Serve with the salad.

Notes:

Broccoli Salad

Ingredients:

1 bunch of broccoli, washed and cut into small florets

½ C. raisins

½ C. sunflowers seeds

¼ C. red onion, diced

5 slices cooked bacon, crumbled

1 C. mayonnaise

¼ C. sugar

1½ T. white vinegar

Directions:

Mix first five ingredients together. Mix mayonnaise, sugar, and white vinegar in a bowl. Pour over broccoli salad, and mix well.

Can you "hold" the broccoli?

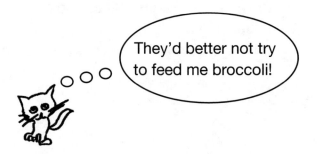

They'd better not try to feed me broccoli!

57

Tomato Salad with Pimentos and Olives

Ingredients:

2 large tomatoes cut into wedges

½ C. Greek style olives

½ C. feta cheese

8 pimentos, small cut (Find this in a jar in the olive section of your grocery store.)

Dressing Ingredients:

¼ C. olive oil

1 T. red wine vinegar

1 T. fresh parsley, minced

1 T. chives, minced

salt and pepper to taste

Directions:

Place the vinegar, parsley, and chives in a bowl. Pour in the olive oil slowly while whisking until combined.

Place the tomatoes on a large plate, overlapping them. Put the olives and pimento slices in the middle. Whisk the dressing mixture together until thoroughly mixed. Drizzle the dressing over the tomatoes, olives, and pimentos. Sprinkle cheese on top.

I'm sure it will be done by the time they get here!

 Serve with whole wheat crackers or rye crisp.

Notes:

Shall I toss the salad to you?

 This is delicious with fresh fruit.

Notes:

Wrap It Up

Oh-So-Easy Lettuce Wraps

Ingredients:

1 small chicken, cooked and cut into small cubes

½ C. onion, diced

½ C. green grapes, diced

¼ t. celery seeds

2 celery stalks, washed and minced

1 garlic clove, minced

½ C. raisins (optional)

½ C. mayonnaise

2 t. curry

1 small Boston lettuce, washed

salt and pepper to taste

Directions:

Bring a 6 qt. pot of water to a boil. Add chicken and boil approximately forty minutes. You will know when the chicken is done when the inside is white, not pink. Let it cool. Pull chicken off bone. In a bowl add grapes, celery, chicken, onions, and raisins. Add spices, garlic, mayonnaise, and mix. Take washed lettuce leaves and fill with ¼ C. chicken salad. Roll over both sides of lettuce and serve.

Chicken Pita Sandwich Wrap

Ingredients:

½ t. fresh dill, chopped fine

½ C. plain yogurt

½ cucumber, peeled and diced into small cubes

4 whole wheat pita pockets, pre-sliced

4 lettuce leaves washed, dried, and torn into pieces

1 tomato, sliced

4 oz. cooked, sliced chicken breast, sliced thin

½ C. feta cheese

1 small red onion, sliced thin (optional)

4 basil leaves, washed

Directions:

To make dressing, combine yogurt, cucumber, and dill; chill for at least one hour. The dressing can be made the day before and kept refrigerated overnight. Take each pre-sliced pita pocket and open it. Put in chicken, tomato, feta cheese, lettuce, and red onion. Top with basil leaf and pour 1 to 2 t. of dressing on top.

 This is very low in fat and delicious.

I fed the kitty this week.

Low Fat Tomato Avocado Cheese Sandwich

Ingredients:

2 slices whole wheat or grain bread

½ avocado, sliced thin

1 slice tomato, sliced round

4 lettuce leaves, washed and dried

1 slice reduced fat mozzarella cheese

2 basil leaves, washed and dried

1 t. mustard

1 t. honey (optional)

Mom will know what a "tomato round" is.

Directions:

Toast both slices of bread. Add cheese to one piece, and broil until cheese bubbles. When cheese has melted, spread the other piece with mustard. Top with the avocado slices, lettuce, and basil leaves. Drizzle honey on top of the basil leaves. Top with second piece of bread.

This is a low fat, healthy, and quick sandwich and a great pick-me-up between classes.

Low Fat Chicken Melts

Ingredients:

4 boneless, thin cut, skinless chicken breasts

1 red onion, cut into ring slices

4 pieces low fat provolone cheese

1 T. deli mustard

1 tomato, cut into 4 slices

4 fresh basil leaves

4 pieces of whole grain or light wheat bread

salt and pepper to taste

2 T. olive oil

Did I remember the cheese?

Directions:

Season chicken with salt and pepper. Put olive oil in a skillet, and let it get hot, but don't let it burn. When the oil is hot, put in the chicken breasts, and cook on each side for five to eight minutes, depending on the size of the breasts. Set aside. Coat a cookie sheet with cooking spray. Put the slices of bread on the sheet, and toast under broiler until slightly brown. When lightly brown, coat each piece with deli mustard. Make open face sandwiches by topping each piece of toast with one piece of chicken, one onion ring, one tomato slice, and one piece of provolone cheese. Place under the broiler until cheese is melted. Top with basil leaf.

Soupy Soups

Healthy Low Fat Pumpkin Soup

Ingredients:

1 30-oz. can of pumpkin puree

½ t. turmeric

½ t. cumin

1 garlic clove, crushed (or garlic buds from a jar can be used)

1 t. low fat sour cream

1 t. chives, chopped

salt and pepper to taste

Directions:

Put all ingredients into a blender and blend until it becomes completely liquidized. Pour into a pan and heat to a slow rolling boil. After it is has boiled, take off heat and let stand for ten minutes.

Serve with a fresh, hot French baguette.

For an impressive dish, slice a pumpkin into two halves and de-seed. Bake at 275 degrees for at least two hours until soft and slightly caramelized. Scoop out the contents and puree in blender until smooth. Follow the same recipe as above with the fresh cooked pumpkin. This recipe can be served as one course with an entrée from the chapter "PhD: Perfectly Hosted Dinners." This recipe is low in fat, inexpensive, and delicious.

Divine Tomato Basil Soup

Did you call me divine?

Ingredients:

1 15 oz. can of fat free chicken stock

2 15 oz. can of tomatoes, whole or diced

1 T. dried basil (double the basil if you use fresh)

1 large garlic clove, minced

¼ C. chives, chopped

1 t. sour cream

salt and pepper to taste

Directions:

Put all the ingredients into a blender and pulse until it is completely liquidized. Pour into a pot and heat to a slow rolling boil. Turn to low and simmer for ten minutes. To serve, add 1 C. soup to bowl, garnish with 1 t. sour cream, and sprinkle some diced chives on top. Serve with a fresh, hot French baguette.

This recipe is already low in fat, but to make it even less fat, substitute fat free sour cream for regular sour cream. It is low in calories, but still very filling.

BA: Breakfast Attitudes

Break the Fast of Overnight

They say breakfast is the most important meal of the day.
It's true because it starts the metabolism moving.

I keep hearing them say "feed the kitty," but I'm still hungry!

Notes:

Granola

Apple, Walnuts, and Cinnamon Granola

Are you sure whole grain tastes good?

Ingredients:

2 C. quick oatmeal

1 C. toasted whole grain cereal

½ C. oat bran

¼ C. walnuts, chopped fine

1 C. dried apples, chopped

2 t. cinnamon

2 T. butter

¼ C. applesauce

¼ C. honey

2 ½ T. brown sugar

Directions:

Combine the first six ingredients in a large bowl; mix well. Melt 2 T. butter in a saucepan over medium heat. Add the applesauce, honey, and brown sugar; then bring to a boil. Cook one minute, stirring frequently. Pour applesauce mixture over dry mixture. Mix well.

Banana, Strawberry, and Blueberry Parfait

Ingredients:

1 C. granola cereal

2 t. coconut, toasted

8 T. low fat strawberry yogurt

½ medium banana, sliced

½ C. strawberries, sliced

½ C. blueberries, fresh or frozen

cooking spray

Directions:

Spray a small skillet with cooking spray, and heat over medium heat. Add the coconut, and cook until toasty brown. Let cool. Place 2 T. yogurt, 1 T. cereal, 1 layer of banana, 1 layer of blue-berries, and 1 layer of strawberries in a parfait glass or any large glass. Continue adding layers until you reach the top. Top with the toasted coconut. Serve immediately.

Wow! That was a home run!

Low Fat Buckwheat Pancakes with Yogurt and Granola Topping

Ingredients:

1 box of buckwheat pancake

4 t. granola cereal

1 container low fat strawberry yogurt

cooking spray

Directions:

Follow directions on box to make four pancakes. If you want more, double the ingredients accordingly. Coat a skillet with cooking spray, and place over medium heat. Using a measuring cup, drop 1/4 C. of batter into the skillet. When bubbles appear on the edges, flip once, and cook one minute or until both sides are golden brown. Put the pancake on the plate, and top with 1 T. of yogurt. Put 1 t. of granola on top of the yogurt. Repeat with each pancake.

Do you think it's supposed to be whole wheat?

Tasty, Toasty Homemade Granola

Ingredients:

5 C. uncooked rolled oats

½ C. wheat germ

1 C. sunflower seeds

½ C. walnuts, chopped

1 C. sesame seeds

1 T. cinnamon, ground

½ C. raisins

½ C. cranberries, dried

1 C. whole-wheat flour

1 T. canola oil

1 C. honey

1 t. vanilla

Actually, it's my mom's granola...

Directions:

In a large bowl, combine all dry ingredients except raisins and cranberries. Add the wet ingredients, and mix well. Place the mixture in a greased casserole dish. Bake at 350 degrees for thirty-five to forty-five minutes, stirring every ten minutes. The longer you cook it, the crispier it will become; so cook it according to the taste you like. When toasted, take out, stir in the raisins and cranberries, mix well, and let cool. Store granola in an airtight container.

Eggs

Egg in a Basket

Ingredients:

1 slice whole wheat bread

1 large egg

1 slice cheddar cheese (optional)

a dash of hot sauce (optional)

2 ½ t. butter or cooking spray

salt and pepper to taste

Directions:

Put 2 t. of butter in a skillet over medium heat. When melted, put in the slice of bread. Cook until toasted, and then flip the bread over. Using the top of a jar or small bottle, cut a hole in the middle of the bread; remove and put the round in the pan. Put remaining ½ t. butter in the hole. Crack the egg into the hole. Cook until the white of the egg is firm on bottom. Flip carefully and cook until all white is done. If you are adding cheese, add to the top after you have flipped the last time. Top with a dash of hot sauce. Salt and pepper to taste.

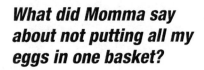

What did Momma say about not putting all my eggs in one basket?

Simply Scrambled Eggs

Who else wants one?

Ingredients:

1 sausage patty

¼ C. water

2 eggs

¼ C. sharp cheese, grated

salt and pepper to taste

cooking spray

Directions:

Spray a frying pan with cooking spray, and place pan over medium heat. Add sausage; brown on both sides. When sausage is brown, add ¼ C. water. Lower heat to a simmer. Cover and cook until no pink remains in the sausage. After sausage is done, beat eggs with a fork in a small bowl. Add a little salt and pepper to the eggs. In another frying pan, cover with cooking spray and place over medium heat. While holding the bowl of eggs over the pan, beat with a fork while pouring slowly into the pan. Shake and poke eggs with spatula for thirty seconds; then stop and let eggs cook. When eggs are almost done, add grated cheese to eggs. Cover and let steam for ten seconds or until cheese is melted. Serve with sausage and your choice of toasted bread.

Pork sausage must be cooked until there is no pink on the inside. When you think it is done, cut one open. If you see pink, cook some more. Also, you must wash your hands when you handle raw pork. Be careful not to cross-contaminate the other food.

Egg and Cheese Sandwich

Ingredients:

1 egg

1 T. white vinegar

2 C. water

1 piece of your favorite bread

1 piece cheddar cheese

hot sauce (optional)

Directions:

Add water and white vinegar to saucepan. Place on medium, and bring to a boil. Reduce heat to a simmer. Crack egg into a small bowl. Using bowl, gently lower egg into simmering water. As egg cooks, gently move water over the egg with a large spoon. Cook egg until the clear part looks white, not transparent. Toast bread in the broiler until slightly brown. Put a piece of cheese on top of the toast, and continue broiling until cheese melts. Top with egg. Dot with hot sauce, salt, and pepper.

 Try and switch to whole wheat or a nine grain bread. It really is good and full of fiber.

What's with the whole wheat thing?

Scrambled Eggs and Sausage Patty on a Bagel

Ingredients:

2 eggs

1 cooked sausage patty

1 slice American cheese

1 bagel

2 drops hot sauce (optional)

salt and pepper to taste

Directions:

In a small bowl, beat two eggs together. Set aside. In a small pan, brown the sausage patty on both sides, add a small amount of water, and cook the sausage until there is no pink. Heat a small pan using cooking spray, and scramble the eggs. Put the sausage patty on one half of a bagel. Top with the cheese, and run under the broiler until cheese is melted. Top the other half with the scrambled egg. Sprinkle with salt and pepper and two drops of hot sauce. Combine two slices of bagel, and enjoy!

What keeps the egg from falling through the hole?

Egg and Bacon Casserole

Ingredients:

4 pieces of bacon, cooked and broken into tiny pieces

4 eggs, slightly beaten

4 slices bread

½ C. milk

1/4 t. paprika

1/4 t. dry mustard

4 t. butter, melted

½ C. scallions, chopped fine

salt and pepper to taste

If he doesn't like this, I don't know what to cook.

Directions:

In a large skillet, fry the bacon until crisp. Drain on a rack or paper towels. Brush the bread slices with a small amount of butter, and cut into slices to fit the bottom of a greased deep casserole dish. Cover the bread with the pieces of bacon. Combine the eggs, milk, scallions, and seasonings; pour over the bread. Bake at 350 degrees for twenty minutes or until the egg mixture looks puffy. Check by inserting a knife in the middle of the casserole. There should be no mixture on the knife when you pull it out.

Notes:

Grits

A Southern Girl Knows Her Grits

Ingredients:

4 C. water

1 C. quick grits

1 C. cheddar cheese, shredded

2 T. butter

½ t. salt

Grits are a food?

Directions:

Bring water to a rapid boil. Stir in grits until they are mixed well in the water. Lower heat to a slow simmer; cover grits with a lid. Let simmer for the amount of time according to package directions. When done, add the cheese, butter, and salt. Mix well.

Notes:

Sausage Cheese Grits

Ingredients:

1 C. ground sausage

4 C. water

1 C. quick grits

3 eggs, beaten

½ C. milk

½ stick butter

1 C. sharp cheddar cheese, grated

salt and pepper

1 T. canola oil

cooking spray

Directions:

Spray a frying pan with cooking spray. Cook sausage in the frying pan over medium heat until completely cooked. There should be no pink. In a separate pot, bring water and salt to a boil. Slowly stir in grits, and mix well. Lower the heat, cover with a lid, and let simmer for the amount of time according to the directions on the package. You will know when they are done when all the water has been absorbed. Beat the eggs in a bowl. Fold the grits into the beaten eggs. To the mixture add the cooked sausage, ½ of the cheese, milk, and butter. Mix well. Grease a casserole dish with the oil. Add the mixture to the dish. Sprinkle the remaining cheese on top. Bake at 350 degrees for twenty minutes or until the eggs are cooked and the cheese is a light brown. Let cool for seven minutes.

Toast and French Toast

Toast Boast

Ingredients:

sliced wheat bread

With each piece of wheat bread use:

1 T. butter

1 T. sugar

¼ to ½ t. cinnamon

This tastes even better on a cold day!

Directions:

Combine butter, sugar, and cinnamon and cook in a small saucepan over low heat. Stir until combined and butter is melted. Spread mixture on bread; place in broiler. Stay with it because it will broil very quickly. When the cinnamon and sugar bubble, it is done. You can make as many pieces as you want. This is delicious with hot cocoa.

Notes:

Grammer's French Toast Casserole: Sweeter Than Brown Sugar, Y'all

Ingredients:

- 1 stick butter
- 1 ½ C. brown sugar
- 1 ½ t. cinnamon
- 1 loaf country white bread
- 8 eggs
- 2 C. milk
- ¼ to ½ C. maple syrup
- ¼ C. powder sugar

They are going to love this!

Directions:

Melt butter in a bowl in the microwave for one minute or until melted. Add brown sugar, cinnamon, and mix until it is a smooth paste. Spread mixture on the bottom of a 9" x13" glass casserole dish. Remove the crust from the bread, and layer the slices of bread on top of the paste mixture. Use extra small pieces of bread to fill in any gaps. Beat the eggs, add the milk, and mix until combined. Pour mixture over the bread. Cover and refrigerate overnight. Remove from refrigerator; let sit for fifteen minutes. Bake for thirty minutes at 350 degrees. Drizzle maple syrup over top, and run under the broiler until bubbly and golden brown. Sprinkle with powdered sugar before serving.

Delicious French Toast with Blueberry Syrup

Ingredients:

½ loaf French bread

2 T. milk or low fat milk

2 large eggs

2 T. sugar

3 T. butter, melted

1 t. vanilla

1 t. cinnamon

1 C. maple syrup

1 C. blueberries

½ C. walnuts, chopped

cooking spray

Come on now, just taste it!

Directions:

Heat oven to 375 degrees. Cut the French bread into 1" slices. In a large bowl, mix the milk, eggs, sugar, butter, vanilla, and cinnamon together. Put the bread slices in the egg mixture, and turn until well coated. Let soak for three minutes. Spray a cookie sheet with cooking spray. Place egg-coated bread on a greased cookie sheet. Place under broiler, and cook two to three minutes. Turn and cook for another two to three minutes or until golden brown. In a small saucepan, put 1 C. of maple syrup; add blueberries, and cook over low heat until blueberries become tender. Pour over the French toast, top with walnuts, and enjoy!

Muffins and Breakfast Bars

Low Fat Blueberry Muffins

Pleeeease walk lightly!

Ingredients:

- 2 C. whole wheat flour
- 1 T. baking soda
- 2 egg whites, beaten lightly
- ¼ C. honey
- ¼ C. canola oil
- 1 ¼ C. blueberries (Fresh are the best, but frozen will do.)
- 1 C. buttermilk

Directions:

Sift the flour and baking soda together in a large bowl. Remember you can sift using your colander with the small mesh holes. Put the flour and baking soda together in the colander. Using a fork, press back and forth until the mixture is sifted in the bowl. In a separate bowl, mix all wet ingredients together. Make a whole in the dry ingredients and pour in the wet mixture. Add the blueberries, and fold the ingredients together until mixed. Pour into greased muffin pan. Bake at 350 degrees for twenty-five to thirty minutes. Test by putting a toothpick in center. If the toothpick comes out clean, they are done.

 If you don't buy buttermilk, you can make mock buttermilk. Use one cup of 2% or whole milk and add 1 t. of white vinegar.

Nutty Banana Muffins

Yes, they're rising!

Ingredients:

2 C. all-purpose flour

¼ C. sugar

1 T. baking powder

½ t. salt

1 C. milk

1/3 C. canola oil

1 egg, beaten

1 C. mashed bananas

½ C. chopped walnuts (optional)

Directions:

Preheat oven to 400 degrees. Grease a twelve-cup muffin pan. Sift together flour, sugar, baking powder, and salt in a bowl; make a whole in the center of mixture. Mix milk, oil, egg, banana, and walnuts. Pour mixture into the hole. Gently mix batter until all is moistened. Don't over mix. Fill muffin cups ¾ full. Bake for approximately fifteen minutes. Muffins are done when you slide a knife into the center, and it comes out clean.

You may use a meshed, small-hole, basket as replacement for a sifter.

Low Fat Banana Nut Bars

I need an energy bar.

Ingredients:

1 C. mashed bananas

½ C. brown sugar

¼ C. honey

1 large egg

½ t. vanilla extract

1 T. canola oil

½ C. all-purpose flour

¼ C. pecans, chopped fine

1 C. quick cooking oatmeal

¼ t. salt

cooking spray

Directions:

Preheat oven to 350 degrees. Using a whisk, mix the first six ingredients together. Add the flour, pecans, quick cooking oatmeal, and salt to the banana mixture. Stir until blended well. Coat an 8" square baking pan with cooking spray. Pour into pan, and bake at 350 degrees for twenty-five minutes. Cool on a wire rack. This makes ten bars.

Apple Crisp

Ingredients:

- 7 apples, sliced thin
- 1 t. cinnamon
- 1 t. nutmeg
- ½ C. water
- 1 C. sugar
- ¾ C. flour
- 7 T. butter, melted

Directions:

Butter a casserole dish, and fill with apples, water, and cinnamon. Mix remaining ingredients together until crumbly. Spread over apple mixture. Bake for thirty minutes at 350 degrees.

 This is delicious when topped off with a scoop of your favorite ice cream.

Notes:

MBA: Munch and Brunch Attitudes

Could an MBA be this easy?

Skinny Dippins'

Cool Yogurt and Cucumber Dip

No double dipping!

Ingredients:

  1 C. plain yogurt

  2 cloves garlic

  ½ cucumber, skinned

  ½ T. olive oil

  1 t. lemon juice

  1 package of pita pockets

Directions:

Mince the garlic. Slice the cucumber in half and scoop out the seeds. Dice the cucumber in small pieces. Mix first five ingredients together. Cut the pita pockets into medium size triangles.

  Use the pita triangles to dip or you can serve with your favorite chips.

Black Bean and Guacamole Quesadillas

Ingredients:

1 small yellow onion

1 15oz. can black beans, drained

1½ t. chili powder

1 t. ground cumin

½ C. water

2 small avocados

2 t. lime juice

2 C. shredded Mexican cheese

6 flour tortillas, 8" in diameter

sour cream

4 T. oil

salt and pepper to taste

These are delicious and so easy to make.

Directions:

In a medium skillet heat 2 t. of oil. Dice the onion into small pieces. Put the onion in the skillet, and cook over medium-low until it is translucent. This is called "sweating the onion." Add the beans, chili powder, cumin, and water. Cook until the water has evaporated. Remove from heat. In a bowl, combine the avocado and lime juice; mix together until it becomes a chunky paste. Season with salt and pepper.

Spread the bean mixture over one flour tortilla. Add the cheese, and top with another flour tortilla. Put remaining oil in a large skillet over medium heat. Place the flour tortilla in the skillet, and cook for one and a half minutes. Then flip and cook an

*Continued on next page

additional one and a half minutes or until cheese has melted. Cut into small triangles. Top with 1 t. avocado mixture and 1 t. sour cream. Repeat with each tortilla. The recipe makes three whole quesadillas. If you want more, mulitply ingredients accordingly.

 To open an avocado, cut in half the long way around. Using a folded dish towel, hold the avocado in your hands and twist apart to separate. Take the pit out and discard. Dice the avocado into small pieces.

Notes:

Momma's Hot Artichoke Dip

Ingredients:

1 14 oz. can of artichokes hearts, drained and chopped

1 C. mayonnaise

1 C. parmesan cheese, grated

1 garlic clove, crushed

salt and pepper to taste

Directions:

Mix all ingredients together except the cheese. Put in a greased Pyrex dish. Top with the cheese. Cook at 350 degrees for twenty-five minutes or until it bubbles. Serve with your favorite chips.

You know it's good; it's my Mom's!

 For a more impressive way to serve, cut the top off of a round loaf of bread. Pull the inside of the loaf out and tear the bread into small pieces. Place the torn bread around the outer crust of the bread. Put the dip in the hole and serve with the pieces of bread and your favorite chips.

There's a Little Salsa in Us All!

Ingredients:

- 1 lb. ground beef
- 2 lb. Velveeta cheese, cubed
- 1½ C. salsa
- 4 drops hot sauce
- 1 package tortilla chips
- 1 package soft flour tortillas, cut into triangles

You expect me to play and cook?

Directions:

In a large frying pan, brown the beef until there is no pink. Drain well. In a saucepan, heat the cheese on low heat until it has melted. This can be heated in a double broiler, by placing one large pot with water and a smaller pot over the water with the cheese in the smaller pot. Add the salsa and hot sauce. If you like it hot, add more hot sauce. Combine the beef and cheese, and then mix. Keep the cheese mixture over a bowl of hot water, or reheat in the micowave for a few seconds until warm.

Serve with tortilla chips and soft tortillas.

Notes:

Bill's Dill Dip

Ingredients:

- ½ C. mayonnaise
- 1 C. sour cream
- 1 T. parsley flakes
- ¼ t. dry mustard
- 1 small bunch fresh dill

Directions:

Chop dill into small pieces. Mix all ingredients together, and chill several hours before serving. Serve with celery sticks and other raw vegetables.

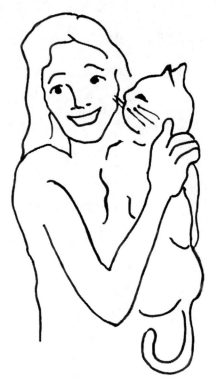

It's not catnip!

Notes:

Skinny on the Dipping with Spinach Dip

Ingredients:

1 pkg. frozen spinach, thawed and drained

1 pkg. of dry vegetable soup mix

2 green scallions, chopped fine

1 C. low fat mayonnaise

1 C. sour cream

salt and pepper to taste

Spinach is good. Really!

Directions:

Place frozen spinach on a plate to thaw. Squeeze the spinach several times to make sure all the water has been drained. Mix all of the above ingredients together and refrigerate overnight.

 Serve with your favorite chips or pita triangles.

Notes:

French Onion Dip

Ingredients:

1 package onion dip

1 C. low fat mayonnaise

½ C. low fat sour cream

1 t. Worcesterchire sauce

a dash of salt and pepper

Directions:

Mix all ingredients together, and serve with your favorite chips.

Notes:

Shrimply Delicious Dip

Ingredients:

- 1 C. sour cream
- 1 package Italian mix

    You will find this in the salad
    dressing section.

- 1 package frozen small salad shrimp
- 1 8 oz. container cream cheese

**Okay, who made the shrimp dip?
I've got to get this recipe!**

Directions:

Thaw the shrimp, and let the rest of the ingredients get to room temperature. Fold together the first three ingredients. Using the back of a spoon, mix the cream cheese until smooth. Fold the cream cheese into the sour cream and shrimp mixture very lightly until mixed.

Serve dip in the hole of a round bread loaf. Also good with Fritos or toasted pita triangles.

Notes:

Wrap and Roll and Seafood Too!

Veggie or Add a Little Meat Wraps

Ingredients:

1 C. cut up vegetables, any that you like

2 slices your favorite deli meat (optional)

2 slices low fat cheese

1 package whole wheat tortilla wraps

1 8 oz. cream cheese

2 T. olive oil

Optional condiments: fresh dill, capers, and/or hot peppers

salt and pepper to taste

It's a wrap!

*Directions on next page

Directions:

Add oil to frying pan, and put over medium heat. Put in the veggies, and cook until slightly tender. Add salt and pepper to taste. Lightly spread cream cheese on two wraps, and then top each with the slice of cheese. You can also use deli meat in the wrap. Put one piece of meat on top of the cheese. You can also add dill, capers, and hot peppers on top. If you don't want capers or hot peppers, the dill on the cream cheese adds a nice flavor. Put the veggies on top. Roll the wrap toward the free end of the wrap. Sometimes you might like to use queso cheese, which can be melted and poured over the veggies. Get creative with this one; it's fun to try new ways to wrap-it-up!

 Where has that kitty been hiding?

Notes:

Salmon Bagels

Ingredients:

- 1 package of smoked salmon
- 1 package low fat cream cheese
- 1 bagel per person
- 1 small bottle capers
- 1 small red onion, sliced thin

Do salmon really swim upstream?

Directions:

Serve one bagel per person. Cut the bagel in half and lightly toast. Spread one half of a bagel with cream cheese. Put one piece of salmon on top of the cream cheese. Add one or two slices of red onion and three to four capers on top. Top with the other half of the bagel. Cut these into quarters when serving for a party.

Try using 100 per cent whole grain. Whole grain is when the entire kernel is still intact. Refined grains have had the bran and germ removed by milling. Whole grains provide fiber, B vitamins, and minerals. Refined grains have been stripped of iron content, fiber, and B vitamins. Whole grains have been shown to help reduce the risk of heart disease and certain types of cancer. Whole grains are also beneficial toward the control of diabetes. Why not try it? You have nothing to lose and a lot to gain!

Curry Shrimp Salad

Ingredients:

1½ lbs shrimp

2 C. noodle shells

2 bunches scallions, sliced

2 apples, skinned and cut into chunks

1½ C. red grapes, sliced

1 C. raisins

1 C. red bell pepper, chopped

1½ C. celery, chopped

1 C. black olives, chopped (optional)

2 t. curry powder (add according to taste)

1 C. light mayonnaise

Salt and pepper to taste

1 small tomato (optional)

1 large iceberg lettuce leaf (optional)

I'm so not there anymore.

 ½ C. Regular mayonnaise mixed with ½ C. reduced fat sour cream makes a great low fat alternative for mayonnaise.

Directions:

Boil shrimp for three minutes or until shrimp is pink. Let cool; remove shrimp shells. When cool, cut into bite-size pieces. Set aside. Cook noodles according to the directions on package. Mix next eight ingredients together with the cooked noodles. Mix with light mayonnaise. Add the shrimp, salt, and pepper to taste. Mix well. Scoop out the middle of a ripe tomato and put salad inside hole. Serve stuffed in a tomato or on a bed of lettuce.

 Ask new friends over; this one is fail-proof.

Notes:

PhD: Perfectly Hosted Dinners

Date Night Dinners, Light Dinners, Late Night Dinners, and Dinner Parties

Main Courses

Easy, Quick, and Yummy Pork Chops

Ingredients:

1 package thin porkchops (bone in)

1 can cream of mushroom soup

1 can of water

2 T. canola oil

1 lemon

salt and pepper to taste

I hope I have the chops to pull this off!

Directions:

Heat oil in a large frying pan. When hot, add pork chops and brown about two minutes on each side. While pork chops are browning, in a saucepan, mix the mushroom soup with one can of water and lemon juice. Squeeze lemon through your fingers to keep seeds out. Heat, stirring occasionally until hot. Pour mushroom soup over pork chops, reduce heat to medium. Continue to cook on top of the stove for five to ten minutes or until the pork chops are done. You can tell when they are done when the inside is white—not pink! If they are pink at all, cook some more.

 To compliment this delicious meal, serve with rice and applesauce.

Momma's Meatballs

Ingredients:

½ lb. hamburger meat

½ lb. ground pork

½ lb. ground veal

1 onion, minced

2 eggs

½ C. bread crumbs

¼ C. milk

1 t. salt

1 t. pepper

4 T. cooking oil

1 t. dried parsley

2 t. Worchester sauce

1 t. Italian seasoning

½ C. brown sugar

1 20 oz. can tomato sauce

1 package spaghetti noodles

1 jar of Parmesan cheese

French bread:

1 loaf of French bread

4 T. butter

1 garlic clove, minced

Hey, who spilled the oil?

*Directions on next page

Directions:

Combine all the ingredients together except the noodles, tomato sauce, brown sugar, and Parmesan cheese. Roll into 2" balls. Heat the oil in a large pan on top of the stove. When oil is hot, put in meatballs, and brown on all sides. When the meatballs are brown, put them in a large, greased casserole dish. Mix tomato sauce, and brown sugar together; pour over the meatballs. Put casserole in a preheated oven at 350 degrees, and bake for thirty minutes. While meatballs are baking, put noodles in boiling water. Cook noodles according to the instructions on the package. Drain the noodles and put in bowls with meatballs on top. Sprinkle with parmesan cheese.

 Serve this dish with garlic French bread. Melt 4 T. of butter in a sauce pan. Add 1 clove of minced garlic; cook until butter is melted. Slice the French bread down the middle, and drizzle the butter mixture on the slit. Wrap in foil and bake at 325 degrees for fifteen minutes.

Notes:

Honey and Rosemary Chicken

Ingredients:

4 chicken breast

½ C. honey

¼ C. lemon juice

2 t. rosemary leaves, crushed

¼ t. red pepper flakes

Chicken juice? A cat can dream, can't he?

Directions:

Wash and pat dry the chicken breast. Place in a greased casserole dish. Combine all of the ingredients to make a sauce, and brush half of mixture over the chicken. Bake at 350 degrees for forty-five minutes. If you don't have a meat thermometer, you can test if it is done by cutting into the chicken. The insides of the chicken will be white and the juices clear. While baking, brush the chicken several times with the remaining sauce. If you use a meat thermometer place it in the thickest part of the chicken, but not touching the bone. The temperature should measure 175 degrees.

Serve with brown rice and a garden salad. This can be used as a dinner, or eat the other pieces of chicken throughout the week on sandwiches or on a salad.

Easy, Crispy Fish Fillets

Ingredients:

1 lb. skinless cod or flounder (This will make two
  servings, unless you're really hungry.)

1 C. flour, cornmeal, or Panko flakes

½ C. buttermilk or use mock buttermilk (1 t. vinegar in
  1 cup milk)

canola oil

tartar sauce

salt and pepper to taste

Let's have fish. I hear it's
good for the brain.

Directions:

Cut fish into desired strips. Put the fish in the cornmeal, shake off excess, dip in the
buttermilk and then again in the cornmeal. Follow same directions if using Panko. In
a large skillet, put about 1/2 inch of canola oil. Raise the heat, which can be tested
by dropping a tiny amount of the flour into the oil. The flour will immediately fry when
the oil is ready. Put several pieces of fish in the pan, and cook until they are golden
brown (about two minutes on each side). Don't crowd the fillets when cooking. When
done, the fish will flake when gently pulled apart with a fork.

Drain the fillets on paper towels.

  Panko is a Japanese bread crumb.

Rice and Pork Chops

Ingredients:

4 pork chops (medium size with bone in)

½ C. white rice

1 t. salt

1 t. pepper

1 onion, sliced thin

1 green pepper, chopped fine

1 can French onion soup

1 can water

1 small can water chestnuts

1 bunch asparagus

1 lemon

I knew I could do it!

Directions:

Place the pork chops in a large, greased casserole dish. Sprinkle the salt and pepper on both sides of the pork chops. Sprinkle the chestnuts, ½ C. of uncooked rice, and sliced onion over pork chops. Sprinkle green pepper on top, and pour one can of French onion soup and one can of water over the pork chops. Bake at 350 degrees for approximately forty-five minutes. (Or if you have a thermometer, the temperature should be 175 degrees.) Wash asparagus and cut the ends off. Place the asparagus in a steamer basket, and steam for three minutes. When cooked, squeeze a lemon through your fingers, over the asparagus, catching the seeds. Serve with a salad.

You can also sauté the asparagus in a pan with a little olive oil. Sprinkle parmesan cheese on top, and cook until cheese has melted.

I've got a secret for you!

Notes:

Hidden Turkey Crouching Mushrooms

Ingredients:

2 C. cooked turkey, diced

¾ C. wild rice, washed and drained

1 C. mushrooms, sliced

4 T. butter

½ C. onions

1 C. cream

1 can of French onion soup

1 can of chicken broth

3 T. parmesan cheese

salt and pepper to taste

Directions:

Preheat oven to 350 degrees. Dice the onions and slice the mushrooms. Brown the mushrooms and onions in 2 T. butter. Put into the bottom of a greased casserole dish. Wash the rice to make sure any dirt or particles have been removed. Add the rice and turkey on top of the onions and mushrooms. Stir the cream, French onion soup, and chicken broth together; and pour over turkey and rice. Add a small amount of salt and pepper. Cover with aluminum foil and bake at 350 degrees for approximately forty-five minutes or until rice is tender. Take off cover, and sprinkle with parmesan cheese and the rest of the butter. Cook an additional ten minutes.

Salad and applesauce compliment this recipe.

Almond Chicken Casserole

Ingredients:

2 C. cooked chicken

1 C. mushrooms

1 small yellow onion

4 T. butter

3/4 C. white rice

½ C. sliced almonds

2 C. chicken broth

1 C. heavy cream

3 T. parmesan cheese, grated

salt and pepper to taste

Pleeeease let it turn out!

Directions:

Dice onions and slice mushrooms. Brown onions in 2 T. butter. When the onions are translucent, add the mushrooms, and cook until tender. When cooked, spread the onions and mushrooms in the bottom of an oiled casserole dish. Place chicken on top of onions and mushrooms. Add all dry ingredients, and stir in the cream and chicken broth. Add the salt and pepper. Cover with aluminum foil, and bake in a preheated oven at 350 degrees for twenty minutes or until bubbly. Remove cover, and top with parmesan cheese and the rest of the butter. Bake an additional ten minutes.

 This goes well with a tossed garden salad.

Sue's Chicken Pot Pie

It's so easy!

Ingredients:

1 whole chicken

1 can celery soup

2 C. chicken broth

1 stick of butter, melted

1 C. self-rising flour

¾ C. buttermilk, or make mock buttermilk below

salt and pepper to taste

 Mix 1 C. milk (2 percent or whole) and 1 t. vinegar to make mock buttermilk.

Directions:

Clean out the cavity of the chicken, and put in a six-quart pot of boiling water for forty-five minutes. When the chicken is done, let cool, and then pull chicken off the bones, discarding skin. Chop into small pieces. Put chicken in a greased casserole. Mix butter with flour, buttermilk, celery soup, and chicken broth; pour over chicken. Bake at 350 degrees for forty minutes or until the top is golden brown.

Gene's Greek Salad

Yes, I've already fed you!

Ingredients:

1 package romaine lettuce, washed, dried
and torn into pieces

16 large black olives

1 package feta cheese, crumbled

16 cherry tomatoes

3 slices of ham, sliced into this strips

low fat Greek salad dressing

4 slices whole wheat bread

1 t. olive oil (per piece of bread)

Parmesan cheese

salt and pepper to taste

Directions:

Combine the first five ingredients. Pour 2 T. of salad dressing over the salad, and mix well. Spread 1 t. of olive oil on each piece of bread; top with parmesan cheese. Cook bread under the broiler until the cheese turns light brown. Enjoy this with your Greek salad. Serves four.

Lucia's Fried Okra

Ingredients:

4 C. fresh or frozen okra

1 C. buttermilk or mock buttermilk

¾ C. all-purpose flour

¾ C. cornmeal

½ C. canola oil

salt

Yes fried, how else would you eat it?

Directions:

If using frozen okra, thaw and drain okra. Put okra in a Ziploc bag with the buttermilk, and shake until all pieces are coated. If you do not have buttermilk on hand, make mock buttermilk by mixing 1 t. of white vinegar to 1 C. of milk. In another bag, add all of the dry ingredients. Put the coated okra into the bag with the dry ingredients, and shake until they are covered. Put the canola oil in a large, deep skillet, and heat on stove top at medium heat. Never fill oil more that ½ to 2/3 high. When oil is hot, gently drop each piece of okra in the oil, and cook until they are crispy and brown. You will want to fry in several batches so that the oil stays hot. When the okra is cooked, remove using a slotted spoon or wire scoop. Place on a wire rack covered in layers of paper towels or in a colander to drain. Salt the okra while they are draining and still hot.

Cute as a Button

Mom was right, they are "as cute as a button!"

Ingredients:

15 large button mushrooms, cleaned and with
  stems removed

½ C. ground sausage

2 T. canola oil, divided

1 egg

½ onion

½ C. herb stuffing mix or seasoned, crushed
  croutons

½ C. parmesan cheese, grated

olive oil

Directions:

Preheat oven to 350 degrees. In a large skillet, heat 1 T. canola oil, add sausage, and cook until brown. Remove the sausage and set aside. Add the rest of the oil to the skillet. Dice the onion and cook until onion looks translucent. Transfer the sausage and onions into a large bowl. Stir in the cheese and stuffing mix. Add egg, and mix well. Cover a baking pan with cooking spray. Brush each mushroom top with olive oil. Cook mushrooms for ten minutes at 350 degrees. Remove from oven and stuff each mushroom to the top with the mixture. Place mushrooms on the baking pan, and put in a preheated oven at 350 degrees. Cook until egg has set and stuffing is crispy.

 In all cases where sausage contains raw pork, it is imperative that the pork is cooked to 175 degrees and there is no pink at all. Also, remember to keep your hands, utensils, and counters clean. Use soap and lots of hot water. Do not use the same utensils you used to cook the pork to serve the pork.

Willie's Buttermilk Biscuits

Ingredients:

2 C. unbleached all-purpose flour

¼ t. baking soda

1 T. baking powder

1 t. salt

5 T. butter, cold

¾ C. buttermilk

College has taught me so much.
It is so much easier kneading dough
this way than how the book tells you to do it!

Directions:

Preheat oven to 450 degrees. Combine all of the dry ingredients together. Cut the butter into small pieces, about the size of a pea. Put the butter in with the dry ingredients. Make a well (hole) in the center, and pour in the buttermilk. Gently blend all ingredients together until it forms small clumps, but do not press too much. Use a fork; you don't want to melt the butter with your hands. If it appears dry, add a little more buttermilk. If it's too wet, add some flour. Place the dough on a floured board. Rub out with your palm until the dough is ½" thick. Using a cookie cutter, cut into circles, and place on a greased cookie sheet. If you don't have a cutter, use the top of a round washed jar or lid. Cook at 450 degrees for ten to twelve minutes.

When handling dough, it is always best to not handle it too much. And try not to turn the cutter as you pull it out of the dough. Over-handling dough will cause the biscuits not to rise as much as they should.

Twice Baked Potatoes

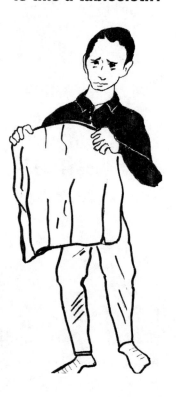

Is this a tablecloth?

Ingredients:

4 medium potatoes

½ C. grated reduced fat cheddar cheese

¼ C. sour cream

3 T. reduced fat bacon bits

¼ C. green onion, minced

Directions:

Scrub potatoes, and pierce with a fork around each potato. Bake in a preheated 400 degree oven until soft, about one hour. When cooked, remove from oven and let them cool Cut potatoes in half lengthwise, and scoop out the centers, leaving ¼" edge around the empty shells and reserving potato flesh. Combine reserve potato, sour cream, and cheddar cheese, and put back in the potato skin shells. Sprinkle bacon bits and green onion on top. Return to the oven, and bake for three minutes or until cheese is melted.

 This is delicious with steak, chicken, or just by itself with a tossed salad.

Dessert

Sue's Simply Delicious Peach Cobbler

Ingredients:

- 1 C. sugar
- 1 C. self-rising flour
- 1 C. milk
- 4 C. peaches, chopped
- 1 stick butter

She thinks this is simple?

Directions:

Melt one stick of butter, and pour in a casserole dish. Pour the peaches in the melted butter. Do not stir. In a bowl, mix flour and sugar together; then add the milk, and mix again. Pour over peaches. Do not stir. Cook at 350 degrees for forty-five minutes or until top is bubbly and brown.

 Your mother would serve this with vanilla ice cream!

Four Courses: One Professor

Pot Luck Dinners

I said "taste," not "test!"

Tomatoes and White Cheese Pizza

Ingredients:

1 large frozen pizza crust or you can buy fresh
    crust in the bakery department of your local store.

2 T. pizza sauce

2 tomatoes, diced

1 C mozzarella cheese, shredded

½ C. ricotta cheese

4 basil leaves, cut into pieces

Move over! It's hot!

Directions:

Preheat oven to 350 degrees. Thaw the pizza crust or if using fresh, roll out by putting a small amount of flour in your hands and press the dough to fit the size of a baking pan. Cover with pizza sauce. Spread the tomatoes evenly on top. Sprinkle the mozzarella cheese on top of the tomatoes. Using small amounts of the ricotta cheese, place in circles around the pizza. Place basil leaves on top of ricotta. Bake for ten minutes or until cheese is bubbly. Add any additional toppings you like. Just make sure they are precooked, such as salami or pepperoni.

Caption: Serve with a salad.

Dijon Chicken Tenders

And to think, I'm really learning to cook!

Ingredients:

¼ onion, cut into slices

1 garlic clove, minced

1 package chicken tenderloins

1 T. dijon mustard

½ C. chicken broth (low sodium)

1 T. olive oil

salt and pepper to taste

Directions:

In a skillet, heat the oil. Sauté onions until translucent. Add minced garlic, and cook another two minutes. Wash and pat dry the chicken and lightly salt and pepper. Add the broth and chicken to the onions, and cook for three minutes on each side. The chicken, when cut, should look white. When the broth has evaporated, remove the chicken and onions to a bowl. Add mustard and mix.

 Serve with applesauce and one of The Dreaded Freshman Fifteen salads.

Soup

Easy French Onion Soup

Ingredients:

½ stick butter

6 medium onions, sliced thin

4 garlic cloves, minced

4 C. chicken stock

1 C. heavy cream

1 bay leaf

4 slices provolone cheese

1 loaf French bread

salt and pepper to taste

Bon appétit!

Directions:

In a large pot, cook onions and garlic in butter over low heat until tender (about one hour, longer if possible). They will have a tan to brown look. Add chicken stock and bay leaf. Season with salt and pepper to taste. Bring to a boil. Lower the heat to a simmer. Cook twenty minutes. Take the bay leaf out, and blend half of the soup in a blender. Add back to the remaining soup. Heat over medium heat. Whisk the cream into the warm soup. Do not let it boil. Cook another five minutes.

Use a good crusty French bread. Cut one piece of bread. Toast in toaster oven, and put in the bottom of soup bowl. Top with one piece of provolone cheese, and pour soup on top. Another fun way to serve this soup is to buy small French baguettes in the deli of your grocery. Cut the tops off, scoop out the bread, put in cheese, and pour the soup in each baguette.

 Serve with a delicious salad.

Notes:

Chicken and Broccoli

This is also known as "Chicken Divan." Use this title when entertaining friends. They will think you really know your way around the kitchen.

Ingredients:

1 chicken cooked and shredded

1 celery stalk with leaves

3 T. olive oil, divided

¼ C. onion, chopped

1 frozen package broccoli spears (thawed and drained)

1 C. sharp cheddar cheese, shredded

1 jar mushrooms

1 can low sodium cream of mushroom soup

1 can low sodium cream of celery soup

2 cans of water

dash of salt and pepper

Don't chicken out. It's easy to make!

Directions:

Clean one whole chicken making sure all the insides are out of the cavity of the chicken. Rinse under cold water. Place the chicken in a large eight-quart pot of boiling water with 1 T. olive oil and celery stalk. Cook chicken until tender, approximately forty-five minutes, or until the chicken falls off the bones by gently separating with a fork. Let cool. As you pull the meat off the chicken, tear into small pieces, discard skin. Sauté onions in 2 T. of olive oil, until the onions look translucent. Add salt and pepper. Drain mushrooms. Add mushrooms and broccoli to sautéed onions, and cook an additional minute. In a sauce pot, add one can of cream of mushroom soup and one can of celery soup with two cans of water. Cook and stir often over medium heat until sauce begins to thicken. In a greased casserole dish, arrange a layer of chicken. Place the broccoli around the chicken pieces. Pour sauce over chicken and broccoli. Sprinkle cheese over the top. Preheat the oven, and bake at 375 degree for twenty minutes until heated throughout and cheese is bubbly.

Notes:

William's Barbecue Pork Roast

Ingredients:

2 lbs. pork roast or shoulder

1 C. beef broth

1 package hamburger buns

1 jar of deli pickles

(Barbecue sauce recipe follows.)

Directions:

In the morning before class, or on Saturday or Sunday, set the Crock-Pot to high heat. Put pork roast in the Crock-Pot. Pour in the beef broth, cover, and let cook for seven hours.

When cooked, take the meat out, drain, and put on a broiler pan or other flameproof shallow pan. Pull the meat apart, and cover the meat with the barbecue sauce. Put in a preheated 450-degree oven for additional ten to fifteen minutes. Serve on plates or on hamburger buns with several pickles.

 Wash your hands, utensils, and the counter after handling raw pork.

Notes:

Bill's Awesome Barbecue Sauce

Ingredients:

2 C. ketchup

1 C. beef broth

½ C. apple cider vinegar

5 T. brown sugar

5 T. white sugar

½ T. onion powder

¼ t. cayenne pepper

¼ C. dry mustard

1 t. lemon juice

1 T. Worchester sauce

1 t. salt

2 t. pepper

There's nothing to it!

Directions:

Mix all of the ingredients together. Stir well. Cook over medium heat until bubbly.

Notes:

Glenn's Spicy Chili

Ingredients:

2 lbs. ground beef

2 lbs. stew meat

2 T. butter

1 T. olive oil

1 16 oz. can whole tomatoes

1 large onion, diced

2 cans kidney beans

2 t. chili powder

¼ t. red pepper

1 t. habanera sauce

1 t. cumin

½ C. shredded sharp cheddar cheese, per bowl

salt and pepper to taste

What's "cumin"?

Directions:

Spray skillet with cooking spray. Cook ground beef in the skillet. While it is cooking, add about ¼ C. of water in the pan so that the meat cooks thoroughly without getting dry. When it is done, drain the fat off the meat. Put the ground beef in a bowl, and set aside. In the same skillet, melt 2 T. of butter. Put in onions, and cook until they look translucent. Take out the onions, add olive oil and stew meat; cook until meat is brown on all sides. Put both meats and onions together in a large pot. Add the canned tomatoes and kidney beans to the cooked meat. Combine all other ingredients together, and add to meat mixture. Add chili powder, salt, and pepper to taste. Cook approximately two hours over low heat. Serve with saltines. Add more habanera sauce or chili powder, if you like it hot. When done, put in bowls, and top with grated cheddar cheese.

 Chili is one of those recipes that the longer it cooks, the yummier it gets. Chili will last in the refrigeratior a good two or three days.

Notes:

Ginger Chicken in Plum Sauce

Ingredients:

4 skinless chicken breasts, cut into 1" strips

1/2 C. plum sauce (Find this in the ethnic section of your grocery store.)

3 T. green onions, sliced

1 T. ginger, grated

3 T. white vinegar

1 package of wooden skewers

Guess what's in the bag?

Directions:

Soak wooden skewers in water. Cut chicken into one inch strips. Mix all ingredients together in a large, plastic, storage bag. Take the chicken out of the marinade, and put three of the chicken strips on a 10" skewer. Repeat on each skewer until all the chicken is used. Put the skewers on a broiler pan. Broil three inches away from the top of the broiler for approximately eight minutes, turning over one time. When cooked, the chicken will be white, not pink! Serve with yellow or brown rice and a garden salad.

Remember to wash your hands after handling raw chicken! Use a plastic cutting board versus a wooden board when cutting or handling meat. Plastic doesn't absorb bacteria; a wooden cutting board can.

Cooking Chicken in the Crock-Pot

Ingredients:

3 carrots, sliced thin

3 celery stalks, sliced thin

1 onion, sliced thin

2 chicken breast, 3 chicken thighs

½ C. chicken broth (use low sodium broth)

1 large potato, peeled and cut into chunks

salt and pepper to taste

Where is everyone?
It was tonight wasn't it?

French bread:

2 garlic cloves, crushed

½ stick butter, melted

1 loaf French bread

Directions:

Put all vegetables in the Crock-Pot, put chicken on top. Pour chicken broth over chicken and vegetables, sprinkle with seasonings. Cook on low for eight hours. Return to a delicious cooked meal that will be perfect for pot luck night!

Cut the French bread down the middle, and pour in the melted butter and crushed garlic. Wrap the bread in foil, and bake at 350 degrees for twenty minutes.

Sweetly Delicious Hawaiian Pork Chops

Ingredients:

4 thin pork chops, bone in

1 T. olive oil

1 8 oz. can of pineapple (save the juice)

1 T. cornstarch

¼ C. chili sauce

¼ C. raisins

1 T. brown sugar

¼ t. cinnamon

1/3 C. chopped dates

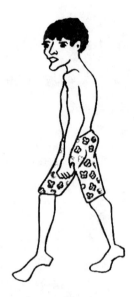

*This is a
LUAU isn't it?*

Directions:

Rinse pork chops, pat dry, and put in a large skillet. In a bowl, combine the pineapple juice with the cornstarch and cinamon. Stir in pineapple, chili sauce, raisins, dates, and sugar. Pour this sauce over the pork chops. For chops that are ¼" thick or less, cover and simmer for ten to fifteen minutes or until pork is thoroughly cooked. If chops are thicker, cook longer.

Notes:

Party Fried Chicken

Ingredients:

10 chicken drumsticks

2 C. all-purpose white flour

½ C. canola oil

salt and pepper

Oh yeah!

Directions:

Rinse chicken legs in cold water, pat dry. Salt and pepper each piece and roll in flour. In a large skillet, heat the oil. When oil is hot, put chicken in skillet, brown both sides of the chicken, keeping oil very hot, but not smoking. When you flip the legs to brown the other side, lower the heat to low, cover the chicken with a top, and cook until done, about thirty-five minutes. When you lower the heat, the chicken will cook at a low sizzle. You can use an electric skillet, but a large skillet on top of the stove will work. After thirty-five minutes, take the top off the skillet and raise heat to medium heat to brown the outer skin.

Notes:

Shrimp with Penne Pasta

Are you sure shrimp come from the sea?
I haven't see one all day!

Ingredients:

1 lb. fresh shrimp

2 T. Old Bay seasoning spice

1 T. fresh basil, chopped

6 T. olive oil, divided

1 T. lemon zest

1 C. frozen peas (use fresh if possible)

1 lb. penne noodles

4 shallots, finely diced

1 garlic clove, crushed

½ fresh hot chile pepper, seeded and minced

2 C. arugula, washed and trimmed in narrow pieces

salt and pepper to taste

Directions:

Bring a six-quart pot of water with Old Bay seasoning to a boil. Drop in the shrimp, and cook about three minutes or until the shrimp looks pink. Drain, let cool; peel and mix with 2 T. olive oil, basil, and lemon zest. To make lemon zest, rub a lemon against a grater, and the peel that comes off is the lemon zest. If using fresh or frozen peas, bring a small pot of water to a boil. Put the peas in, and cook for three minutes. Drain

136

and cool. Bring a large six-quart pot of water to a boil. Cook noodles according to instructions on package. Drain and mix with 1 T. of olive oil. Heat the remaining 3 T. oil in a medium size skillet. Add the shallots, garlic, arugula, and chile pepper. Cook until the shallots are slightly brown and the arugula is wilted. In the pot with the pasta, add the shrimp, shallots, peas, and arugula. Season with salt and pepper.

 When cleaning the Chile pepper, be sure to remove all the seeds and the white membranes and wash, wash, wash your hands. The juice from the pepper is very hot, so you will want to make sure it is off your hands before you touch your eyes!

Notes:

Sides

For the French bread:

Ingredients:

1 loaf of French bread

2 cloves garlic, crushed

½ stick butter

Directions:

In a saucepan heat 1/2 stick of butter and two garlic cloves crushed. Remember you can by garlic buds in a jar. Cut a loaf of French bread down the middle and pour the butter and garlic in the slit, wrap it in foil and bake at 325 degrees for twenty minutes.

Notes:

Do You Think I Just Rolled in on the Back of a Turnip Truck?

It's a Southern thing!

Ingredients:

5 lbs. turnip greens

1¾ lbs. ham hocks (2 large hamhocks)

1½ C. water

1 C. onion, chopped fine

1 qt. low sodium chicken broth

salt and pepper to taste

1 bottled jar of pepper in vinegar to taste

Directions:

Cut off and discard the tough stems and discolored leaves from the turnip greens. Wash the turnip greens in a large bowl of water. They are easier to thoroughly clean by washing them in the kitchen sink. Turnips can hold a lot of dirt, so make sure that each leaf is clean. Tear the leaves to 3"x3" pieces. Put the turnips and the chicken broth in a large pot, and then cover with the water. Clean the ham hocks and put in with the turnips. Add the onion, salt, and pepper. Heat to a slow boil. Cover and cook about forty-five minutes or until the greens are tender. You may need to add more salt and pepper. When the turnips are cooked, cut off any meat from the hocks. Put the meat in the turnips. Drain the water and put turnips in a large bowl. Sprinkle pepper in vinegar on top. Serve with cornbread.

 Before you place the turnips in the sink, be sure to scrub with a cleaner and rinse the sink with lots of water until all the cleaner has been removed.

Aunt Ella's Corn Fritters

Ingredients:

1¾ C. all-purpose flour

2 t. baking powder

½ t. salt

1 egg, slightly beaten

1 C. milk

1 T. butter, melted

2 C. whole kernel corn

2 T. canola oil

Do you need any help with those fritters?

Directions:

In a large skillet heat the oil. While the oil is getting hot, combine all of the ingredients except the corn, blending until smooth. Using a large spoon, slowly fold the corn into the wet ingredients. Drop by spoonfuls into the hot oil. Cook until they are brown, turning to brown on both sides. If you need to use more oil while cooking, add 1 T. at a time.

Notes:

Roasted Asparagus Tips

Ingredients:

1 bunch of asparagus

3 T. olive oil, divided

1 C. fresh Parmesan, shaved

1 lemon, juiced

salt and pepper to taste

Directions:

Heat the oven to 400 degrees. Rinse the asparagus, and cut off ½" off the bottom. In a bowl, toss the asparagus with 2 T. of olive oil, salt, and pepper. Place on a flat, greased baking sheet. Cook for five minutes, and then turn over. Sprinkle with the remaining 1 T. olive oil. Cook for an additional five minutes. Remove and sprinkle with the lemon juice. Lay the shaved Parmesan on top and serve.

You have got to be kidding. You eat them?

Notes:

Are You Sure Its Upside Is Down?

Topping Ingredients:

4 T. butter

¾ C. brown sugar, firmly packed

7 slices of pineapple (You can use canned pineapple slices, drained well.)

Topping Directions:

Melt the butter in a saucepan. Add brown sugar, and cook over moderate heat for three minutes. Remove from heat, and pour into greased 9" round cake pan. Arrange the pineapple slices on top of brown sugar, overlapping them in a circular pattern. Let sit for two minutes.

Cake Ingredients:

½ C. butter

½ C. sugar (white)

1 egg

1½ C. all-purpose flour

1½ t. baking powder

½ t. salt

½ C. milk

It doesn't look upside down to me!

Cake Directions:

Preheat oven to 375 degrees. Cream the butter. (Using a hand beater, blend until the butter looks creamy.) Add the sugar slowly until the sugar and butter are light and fluffy. Add egg to sugar mixture, and beat well. Sift all dry ingredients together. You can sift using your fine screen colander. Put all ingredients into colander over a bowl, and using a fork, go back and forth over the ingredients until it is sifted into the bowl. Add the sifted ingredients, alternating with milk to the creamed sugar, egg, and butter mixture. End with the dry ingredients and mix well. Pour over the pineapple mixture. Bake at 375 degrees for thirty-five minutes. When cool, turn over onto a plate.

 You can use a yellow cake mix and top with the same topping to make things easier.

Notes:

Joanie's Apple Fritters

Ingredients:

1 C. all-purpose flour, sifted

1½ t. baking powder

¼ C. sugar

1 t. nutmeg

1 t. salt

1 egg, beaten

1/3 C. milk

1 T. butter, soft

2 large apples

1 qt. canola oil, for frying

These apples will make the best fritters!

Directions:

Sift together flour, baking powder, sugar, nutmeg and salt. Combine egg and milk; add to sifted flour. Beat until smooth. Add butter, and mix well. Peel and core the apples, and cut into eight thin wedges. Dip the apples in the batter. Put the oil in a deep skillet. When the oil is hot, put in the apples. Cook on each side two minutes or until they are golden brown.

Notes:

Variations on a Theme

Theme Parties, Tailgate Parties,
Holiday Parties, and Late Night Foods

It's all Greek to Me!

Main Courses

Pizza Pinwheels

Ingredients:

- 1 package whole wheat pita pockets
- 1 lb. deli ham
- 1 lb. deli pepperoni
- 1 lb. salami
- 1 small onion, diced
- 2 C. mozzarella cheese, shredded
- 1 green pepper, diced
- 1 large tomato, diced
- 2 t. dried basil (or fresh basil, if available)
- 2 T. butter

Oh man! I forgot to make the pizzas.

Directions:

Cut pitas in half. Place on an ungreased cookie sheet, and cook at 425 degrees for five minutes or until crisp. Turn pitas once while they are cooking. While pitas are cooking, melt butter in a saucepan, and cook onions in butter until clear. Stir the onions so they don't get overcooked. Take each pita half and fill with a portion of the cooked onions, ham, pepperoni, salami, tomatoes, and green pepper. Sprinkle basil on top, and cover with mozzarella cheese. Stand the pitas up by leaning them together. Bake until cheese is bubbly.

 These pizza pinwheels can be topped and cooked with any of your favorite precooked meats.

Notes:

Greek Chicken Kabobs

Ingredients:

4 chicken breast, cubed

1 green bell pepper, cut into 1"x 1" pieces

1 large onion

12 cherry tomatoes

12 mushrooms, washed, stems removed

1 t. oregano

5 T. olive oil, divided

1 package wooden skewers, soaked in water

1 t. paprika

It's always Greek to me.

Directions:

Soak wooden skewers in water for five minutes. Put chicken, oregano, salt, pepper, and 2 T. olive oil in a bowl. Marinate for one hour or longer if possible. Put chicken on skewers by itself. Discard the marinade. Cut onion in half, and then cut each half into quarters. Put onions on a separate skewer, and cook while cooking chicken. Cook on high heat on a grill for about fifteen minutes, turning once. Put the green peppers, mushrooms, and tomatoes on other wooden skewers. Do not let the raw chicken touch the vegetable skewers. While the chicken is cooking, the last seven minutes, cook the vegetable kabobs. Combine 3 T. olive oil and paprika and brush on the kabobs during the last three minutes. The chicken and vegetables should all be done at the same time. This is also delicious with sirloin steak.

If you don't have a grill, these can be cooked in your oven under the broiler. Set broiler on high, and cook according to the directions above. Turn over one time. Just keep an eye on it at all times.

Notes:

Greek Sausage, Onions, and Peppers

Ingredients:

1 garlic clove, crushed

2½ T. olive oil

1 medium onion, sliced

2 whole green or red bell peppers, seeded, and
chopped

3 lb. hot pork sausage, links

2 medium tomatoes, chopped fine

1 hoagie roll per sandwich

1 slice provolone cheese per sandwich

*My Uncle Nick puts this
on a Kaiser roll. Go figure!*

Directions:

Preheat oven to 375 degrees. In a skillet over medium heat, heat the oil and cook onions until they are translucent. Remove from pan. Put sausage in the hot pan and cook for twenty-five minutes or until sausage is completely cooked. When cooked, add the tomatoes and peppers in with the cooked sausage. Add the onions, and cook all together for another five minutes. Put in the garlic, and cook all together an additional two minutes. Depending on how many rolls you are serving, put the ingredients into each hoagie roll, and top with the cheese. Put each stuffed hoagie back in the oven until cheese is bubbly.

Chicken Kabobs with Pineapple

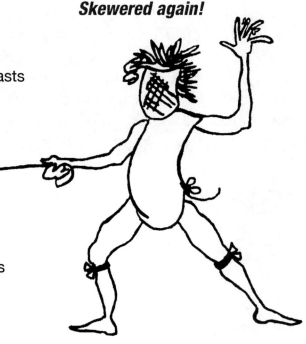

Skewered again!

Ingredients:

1 large package boneless chicken breasts

½ C. cooking oil

½ C. teriyaki sauce

2 garlic cloves, minced

3 t. sugar

2 large onions, cut in half and then
    cut each half in quarters

2 green peppers, cut into 1"x 1" pieces

15 cherry tomatoes

1 can of pineapple, chopped

salt and pepper to taste

1 package wooden skewers

Directions:

Soak wooden skewers in water for five minutes. Rinse chicken, and cut into cubes. Put cubed chicken in a casserole dish. In a bowl, combine oil, teriyaki, garlic, and sugar, and pour over chicken. Marinate in the refrigerator for at least one hour while you are preparing the other ingredients. If you have time, marinate longer, even all day while you are in class. Cut onions into quarters and green peppers into one inch by one inch strips. Put the onions on one skewer and the green peppers on another skewer; cherry tomatoes and pineapples on other skewers. Put chicken on separate

*Continued on next page

skewers. Put the left over marinade in a pot and bring to a boil on the stove. Do not allow raw chicken to touch the vegetables or fruit skewers. Salt and pepper to taste. Preheat grill to medium/high heat. Lightly grease the grate. Put chicken skewers first on hot grill, cooking for ten to twelve minutes, turning over once halfway through. Baste the chicken while cooking with the boiled marinate. Put vegetables on after five minutes and fruits after seven minutes, so all the food will be done together. If you don't have a grill, place the skewers on a cooking sheet and put them in your stove's broiler three inches from broiler top for ten minutes, turning once. Follow the directions above. Serve with white rice, or use yellow rice for more color.

 Remember to wash your hands after handling raw chicken. For easy maintenance and fresher tasting food, clean the grill by scraping off excess after each use.

Notes:

Chicken Tortilla Soup

What goes in Momma's salsa?

Ingredients:

1 whole chicken

4 corn tortillas

1 t. oil

2 14 oz. boxes low sodium chicken broth

2 tomatoes, chopped

1 onion, sliced thin

1 garlic clove, crushed

2 celery stocks, cut into large pieces

1 C. frozen corn

1 C. Monterey Jack cheese

1 jalapeño pepper, sliced into thin strips, optional

1 avocado, sliced thin

 Remember to wash and rewash your hands after touching the pepper. You definitely don't want to get this in your eyes! Ouch! You can also use throw-away latex gloves.

Directions:

Fill a large eight-quart pot with enough water and chicken broth to cover the chicken, bring to a slow boil for forty five minutes or until a leg can be gently pulled apart. When cooked, drain and let cool. Strain the chicken stock through a colander into another large pot to remove any fat. Put the cooked stock back on the stove on medium heat. Separate the meat from the cooked chicken and add to the broth, discard skin. To clean the pepper, cut the pepper in half lengthwise, remove all of the white seeds, and the white membranes inside the pepper, set aside. Add the onions, garlic, celery, tomatoes and corn to the stock then cook together for thirty minutes or until vegetables are tender. Cut the tortillas into strips, and toss with one t. oil. Place the tortilla strips on a baking sheet, and cook in a preheated oven at 400 degrees for five minutes or until they are crispy. Put soup in bowls. Top with cheese, tortilla strips, several pieces of sliced jalapeno pepper and two pieces of sliced avocado in each bowl.

Notes:

Lentils with Kielbasa Sausage

I carry all the weight around here!

Ingredients:

1/2 package lentils, rinsed and drained

2 C. beef broth

1 package turkey kielbasa, cut into ¼" pieces

1 12 oz. can tomatoes

1 garlic clove, minced

1 carrot, diced

½ t. dried oregano leaves

½ t. thyme

salt and pepper to taste

cooking spray

1 loaf of French bread

½ stick butter

2 garlic cloves, crushed

Directions:

In a pot, add lentils to the beef broth. Bring to a boil. While lentils are boiling, spray a skillet with cooking spray and heat the kielbasa sausage and carrots. Add sausage, carrots tomatoes, minced garlic, oregano, and thyme to the lentils. Cook for thirty minutes or until lentils are soft. While lentils are cooking preheat oven to 350 degrees. In a small skillet, melt the butter, and add minced garlic. Cut the French bread down the middle, and pour in the melted butter and garlic. Wrap bread in foil and cook for twenty minutes.

Serve with garlic bread. Perfecto!

That bird sure had a lot of feathers.

 I never met a turkey I didn't like.

Turkey Talk

How to buy a turkey: Plan on 1 lb. of uncooked turkey per person. If you buy a frozen turkey, remember it takes up to three or four days to thaw. When thawing a frozen turkey, place the turkey in its original wrappings in a shallow pan on the bottom shelf of the refrigerator. Allow twenty-four hours per five pounds of turkey. If you decide to buy a fresh, unfrozen one, buy it no more than two days before cooking. Always look at the expiration date for safe cooking.

Cook Until the Turkey Talks

Turkey Size	Hours Un-Stuffed	Hours Stuffed
8 — 12 lbs.	2 ¾ — 3	3 — 3 ½
13 — 14 lbs.	3 — 3 ½	3 ½ — 4
15 — 18 lbs.	3 ¾ — 4 ¼	4 — 4 ¼

Clean out the cavity of the turkey. Place turkey breast side up on a rack in a large roasting pan. (You can buy a throw-away roasting pan in the baking section of a grocery store). Cover the turkey with a loose covering of foil. Roast turkey at 325 degrees until a meat thermometer reaches 175 degrees at the thigh and 165 degrees at the breast. Uncover turkey the last hour to brown. You can baste throughout the cooking process by scooping up the juices with a large spoon and dripping them over the bird. Serve this with Daddy's Cornbread Stuffing on page 167.

When testing the temperature of a bird, insert the tip of the thermometer into the thickest part of the thigh. Make sure the end is angled toward the body but is not touching any bone.

Dips

Black Beans and Chopped Avocado Dip

Ingredients:

1 ripe avocado, diced

1 16 oz. can black beans, drained

3 medium tomatoes

1 8 oz. can corn

½ C. red onion

1½ C. salsa

3 T. lime juice

2 T. olive oil

1 t. sugar

I've been making this since the fifth of May!

Directions:

To prepare, take the seed out of the avocado and scoop out the meat into a bowl. Dice the onion and tomatoes. Combine avocado, beans, tomatoes, corn, and onions. Mix salsa, lime juice, olive oil, and sugar together, and pour over the avocado and bean mixture. Chill for two to three hours. Serve with your favorite tortilla chips.

You can make this the night before. Cover it very tight and refrigerate.

Brittany's Scrumptious Crab Dip

Ingredients:

1¼ C. mayonnaise

1 C. crabmeat (You can use canned crab, picked through to make sure there are no shells.)

½ C. cheddar cheese, grated

1 T. horseradish

4 T. French dressing

Directions:

Mix all the ingredients together, and serve with your favorite crackers or corn chips.

Leftovers make great crab cakes. Take dip, add bread-crumbs, and form into a small cake; fry several minutes on both sides.

***All the studying, test dates, papers due,
and this crazy curriculum make me so crabby.
Am I the only one who feels this way?***

If they don't feed me soon, they'll wish I was a crab!

Lumpy Crab Dip

Ingredients:

1 8 oz. cream cheese

1 8 oz. jar cocktail sauce

1 6 oz. lump white crab meat

½ C. green onions, diced small

1 t. Worcesterchire sauce

½ C. sour cream

2 T. mayonnaise
dash of hot sauce

I can never pass up anything with fish.

Directions:

Set the cream cheese in a bowl until it becomes soft. Spread the cream cheese in a small casserole dish on the bottom and one inch up the sides. Pour the cocktail sauce over the cream cheese. Drain the crabmeat if you are using crab from a can. Mix crab and the rest of the ingredients together, and pour over the cocktail and cream cheese mixture. Chill one hour before serving. Serve with your favorite crackers.

Notes:

Mexican Bean Dip

Ingredients:

- 4 cans refried beans
- 2 pkgs. dry taco seasoning mix
- 2 12 oz. sour cream
- 1 C. shredded cheese
- 1 t. butter

Why are my Mexican beans jumping?

Directions:

Mix together all ingredients. Put in a buttered baking dish. Bake twenty-five minutes at 350 degrees.

 This is delicious when served with corn chips.

Notes:

Onion Dip

Ingredients:

1 package dried onion dip

½ C. mayonnaise

¼ C. sour cream

1 round loaf sourdough bread

salt and pepper to taste

Directions:

Mix the first three ingredients together. Cut the top off the bread, and pull out the inside of the bread. Put the onion dip into the hole in the bread. Tear the bread that you took out into pieces, and display around the loaf. If you are planning on a large crowd, double this recipe.

Should I serve bread and chips?

Sides

Black-Eyed Peas with Ham Hocks:
A Southern Sunday Side Dish

Ingredients:

2 C. dried black-eyed peas

1 lb. meaty ham hocks

6 C. water

1 medium onion, chopped

¼ t. garlic powder

salt and pepper to taste

What part of the pig are hocks?

Directions:

Put peas in a colander, and rinse. Soak peas in a bowl for one hour. In a large pot, bring the water to a boil. Add the onions, peas, and ham hocks. Add the spices, and cook at a gentle boil for one hour. When the peas are tender (keep checking them so they don't get soggy), take the ham hocks out, and pull the meat off. Then add ham back into the peas, discarding the skin.

Serve with cornbread. Cook according to directions on the package.

Greek Yogurt Cucumber

Ingredients:

2 medium cucumbers

1 garlic clove, minced

1 T. white vinegar

2 T. olive oil

1½ t. chopped dill (Fresh dill is best.)

4 green onions, chopped

2 C. plain yogurt

It is too a cucumber!

Directions:

Peel cucumbers, and cut in half lengthwise. Clean out the seeds, and dice the cucumber. Place cucumbers in a colander over a bowl and sprinkle with salt. Let sit in the refrigerator for one hour to drain the water from the cucumbers. Wash off the salt, and mix all ingredients together except the yogurt. Blend in the yogurt with the cucumber mixture. Cover and chill three hours. This can be made the night before and is delicious served on lettuce leaves or pita bread. Toast the pita pockets, and then cut into triangles.

This makes a great party dip.

Cayden's Bruschetta with Goat Cheese, Figs, and Honey

Ingredients:

1 12" loaf baguette, cut into 1/2" slices

2 logs (4 oz) goat cheese

4 whole ripe figs, diced

clover honey to drizzle

What do you mean? It comes from a goat?

Directions:

Heat oven to 400 degrees. Place baguette slices in single layer on baking sheet. Bake eight to ten minutes, or less until crisp, turning each slice once until golden around edges. Let cool. Spread cheese on toasted baguette slices. Top with figs, and lightly drizzle with honey.

 Each baguette loaf will yield about twelve servings.

Fried Cheese Sticks

Ingredients:

1 lbs. part skim milk mozzarella cheese

½ C. flour

4 eggs, beaten

1 C. dry bread crumbs

canola oil

Directions:

Cut cheese so that each piece is approximately the same size stick. Place in flour, and then shake off excess flour. Dip into beaten eggs and into the bread crumbs. Press the crumbs onto the cheese sticks. Dip in the eggs and bread crumbs again until you have a firm coating. Put one inch oil in a skillet on medium heat. When oil is hot, put in four cheese sticks, and cook until they become brown. Turn them once while they are cooking. Be sure to not overcook them. Remove from oil, and place on several paper towels to drain. You can triple this recipe for a party or make as many as you need.

Say cheese!

Daddy's Cornbread Stuffing

Ingredients:

Seven pieces of day-old bread

½ C. chicken broth

7 T. melted butter

3 celery stalks, diced small

2 medium onions, diced small

½ t. dried thyme

1/8 t. ground cayenne pepper

1½ t. salt

2 C. yellow cornmeal

2 C. buttermilk

4 large eggs, lightly beaten

2 t. sage

I put everything in but the kitchen sink!

Directions:

Preheat oven to 350 degrees. In a large bowl, crumble the bread slices and set aside. Melt butter in a skillet over medium heat. Add celery and onions, and cook until the onions are translucent (about seven minutes). Combine the bread with the stock and all remaining ingredients. Add sage, salt, and pepper; mix well. Stuff as much of the stuffing that will fit into the turkey. The rest can be cooked in an oven-proof bowl. When the turkey is done, so is the stuffing that is in the bird. The stuffing in the bowl will cook faster. Cook to an internal temperature of 165 degrees.

Cramming Your Cranium

Foods that Keep the Brain Waves Movin':
Snacks, Study Food, and Smoothies

When You Have to Cram Your Cranium, Enjoy Any of These Healthy Snacks

- beef jerky

- canopies: small sandwiches. Take one piece of ham and one piece of cheese, and put on one side of bread. On the other piece, use 1/4 t. mayonnaise. Cut the crust off, and cut into four triangles. These can be made with turkey, salami, or any of your favorite meats.

- carbonated soda with fresh lemon juice

- celery sticks stuffed with soft cheese, peanut butter, or pimento cheese. Remember to de-vein the celery by breaking the top off and pulling down the stock.

- deviled eggs

- fruit such as mangos, oranges, grapes, strawberries, blueberries, blackberries, and raspberries when in season

- Mix together any combination you like of these: cashews, peanuts, walnuts, almonds, shelled sunflower seeds, pumpkin seeds, chocolate bites

- one handful of peanuts mixed with raisins

- sliced apples topped with peanut butter

- sliced apples with mozzarella slices

- whole wheat pretzels with spicy mustard

- your favorite cheese with crackers

Notes:

Roasted Almonds

Ingredients:

2 C. water

2 C. sugar

4 C. almonds

Directions:

Put all ingredients in a large frying pan. Cook over medium heat until sugar forms a hard shell on nuts (crystallizes) and all water has evaporated. Pour all ingredients onto a cookie sheet, and bake in oven at 350 degrees for twenty minutes.

I can't remember why almonds are good for you.

Salads benefit from the addition of roasted almonds.

These healthy snacks are not good for kitties.

Cucumbers with Fresh Dill

Ingredients:

3 cucumbers

½ C. yogurt, plain and low fat

1 T. fresh dill, diced

salt and pepper

Directions:

Peel the cucumbers. Slice down the middle, and using a teaspoon, remove the seeds. Cut the cucumbers diagonally into ½" slices. Put in a colander over a bowl, and sprinkle with salt. Let the cucumbers sit in the refrigerator for one hour. Rinse, pat dry, and put cucumbers in a bowl with the yogurt and the diced dill, salt, and pepper. Mix well, and put back in the refrigerator for thirty minutes before serving.

I got all the cucumbers and fresh dill they had!

Healthy Avocado and Tomato Slices

Ingredients:

2 small ripe avocados (Ripe ones will be a little soft to the touch, but not mushy.)

1 medium tomato

2 t. olive oil

4 t. lemon juice

2 leaves of basil

salt and pepper to taste

We'll be back with the avocados in a flash!

Directions:

Slice each avocado lengthwise around the whole avocado. Twist and pull apart. Remove the seed in each avocado. Use a spoon to separate avocado from skin. Cut into long pieces, ¼" thick. Place the pieces on a plate, and squeeze the lemon juice over the avocado strips. Squeeze each piece of a lemon wedge through your fingers to catch the seeds. Wash the tomato, and cut it into wedges. Place the wedges on the plate with the avocados. Wash two pieces of fresh basil. Pat dry, and dice into small pieces. Top the tomato wedges with olive oil and fresh basil. Salt and pepper to taste.

This makes a wonderful pick-me-up snack when studying.

Cucumber Circles Topped with Hummus and Yogurt

Ingredients:

2 cucumbers, skin removed

½ C. hummus

½ C. plain yogurt

2 T. honey

3 T. sesame seeds, toasted

3 T. salt

Now that is real "art."

Directions:

Skin the cucumbers with a vegetable peeler. Cut the cucumbers crosswise into ¼" rounds. Put the cucumbers in a bowl, and sprinkle them with salt. Put them in refrigerator, and let sit until the water is released from the cucumbers, about one hour. In a bowl, mix the yogurt with the honey. Take out the cucumbers, rinse the salt off and pat dry. Place 1 T. of hummus on each piece of cucumber. Top with 1 t. yogurt, and sprinkle 1/3 t. of toasted sesame seeds. Repeat until all the cucumber tops are covered. Chill and serve.

Notes:

Awesome Hoagie

Ingredients:

1 lb. salami

1 lb. ham

1 lb. pastrami

1 lb. provolone cheese

mayonnaise to taste

mustard to taste

lettuce

20 slices of tomatoes

10 large hoagie or submarine rolls

salt and pepper to taste

vinegar

canola oil

Will this feed the whole study group?

Directions:

Slice hoagie rolls lengthwise. Put 1 t. mayo and 1 t. mustard on bottom piece of each roll. Layer with lettuce, tomato slices, and two slices of each piece of meat. Top with the slices of cheese. Season with salt, pepper, and a dash of vinegar and oil on each sandwich.

Cut the hoagie rolls into six-inch slices, and serve on a large platter. Chips, dips, and salsa are great fill-ins for large groups of friends.

I said, "That is the perfect amount for me!

Falafels in Pita Pockets

Ingredients:

1 package falafel mix

6 small package pita pockets

1 C. Greek yogurt

2 T. lemon juice

6 t. parsley, chopped

½ cucumber, diced

¼ t. garlic powder

¼ t. salt and pepper

Exercise will set you free!
You can eat what you want, within reason.

Directions:

Make the falafel balls according to the instructions on the box. Set aside. Peel the cucumber, slice length wise in two, remove the seeds. Dice the cucumber. Put diced cucumber in a colander, and place a heavy saucepan on top to drain all the water out of the cucumber for twenty minutes. In a bowl, mix the Greek yogurt, cucumber, lemon juice, garlic powder, salt, and pepper. Open up each pita pocket. Put two falafel balls in each one, and top with 1 T. of the yogurt mixture. Top with one t. of chopped parsley.

Spinach and Artichoke Dip

Ingredients:

1 bottle or can artichoke hearts, in water or oil

1 10 oz. package frozen spinach

1/3 C. low fat cottage cheese

1 C. low fat sour cream

1 C. parmesan cheese

2 garlic cloves, crushed

cooking spray

I think I need to eat more veggies...

Directions:

Put frozen spinach in a colander; thaw and drain until all water has been removed. It helps to put a heavy saucepan on top to allow all the water to drain out of the spinach. Put the cottage cheese and artichokes in a blender, and blend until slightly chunky. Add sour cream, garlic, spinach, and parmesan to the cottage cheese and artichokes; blend all ingredients twenty or thirty seconds. Put all the ingredients in a greased casserole dish. Cook for twenty minutes in a 350 degree oven.

Serve with crisp pita chips or any of your favorite chips.

Notes:

Mix and Match Slushies and Smoothies

Peanut Enhanced Smoothie

Ingredients:

½ banana

1 C. low fat milk

1 T. honey

1 t. peanut butter

1 t. wheat germ

4 ice cubes

Does stomping on peanuts make peanut butter?

Directions:

Combine all ingredients in a blender; blend until smooth and creamy.

Notes:

Berry Smooth

Ingredients:

½ C. strawberries

½ C. raspberries

¼ C. plain yogurt, low fat

¼ C. milk, low fat

¼ C. sugar or sugar subsitiute

½ t. wheat germ

6 ice cubes

This was a smooth move!

Directions:

Put all ingredients in a blender, *cover*, and blend until smooth.

Notes:

Watermelon Slush

Ingredients:

4 ½ C. seeded watermelon, cubed

1 small package of fresh raspberries

¼ t. sugar substitute

1 12 oz. bottle of sparkling water

½ C. ice cubes

Two pieces of fresh mint for each slushy (optional)

Directions:

Put watermelon and raspberries in a blender, add the sparkling water and ice cubes, and blend together. Add 1/4 t. sugar substitute and blend. Pour into tall, chilled glasses. Top with a sprig of mint.

This sure is sticky!

Orange Creamsicle

Ingredients:

- 1 C. skim milk
- ½ C. orange juice
- ½ t. vanilla extract
- 1 C. of ice cubes

Directions:

Mix all ingredients together in a blender and put on high until the ice becomes slushy.

Notes:

Lemon Orange Tea

Ingredients:

1½ C. ice tea

1/8 C. lemonade

1/8 C. orange juice

Directions:

Mix all ingredients together. Blend well.

I'm waiting.

Notes:

Banana Crunch

Ingredients:

1 C. skim or reduced fat milk

2 marshmallows

3 T. chocolate syrup

1 banana

2 T. granola for topping

whipped cream for topping

Directions:

Mix all ingredients together (except whipped cream and granola) together in a blender until smooth. Put a dollop of whipped cream and granola on top.

Notes:

Tropical Slushy

Ingredients:

- 2 oz. pineapple juice
- 2 oz. lemon juice pulp
- 4 oz. grape juice
- 4 oz. lemon-lime soda
- 1 C. ice

Directions:

Put ingredients in blender. Blend and enjoy!

Notes:

Orange Juice Slushy from the Good Ole Days

Ingredients:

1 can frozen orange juice

¼ C. sugar

4 C. ice

Directions:

Mix the orange juice with the right amount of water. Add 8 oz. of orange juice to a blender. Fill the blender with as much ice as it will hold. Add sugar, and blend on high until ice is crushed.

This drink is perfect for a pick-me-up between classes.

 To lower the sugar amount, you can substitute the sugar with an artificial sweetner. Artificial sweeteners are much sweeter tasting than real sugar, so try adding a small amount in the orange juice to find the sweetness level that is right for you.

This is way better than I remember.

Low Fat Yogurt Slushy

Ingredients:

- 1 C. low fat yogurt
- 1 ripe banana
- ½ C. fresh strawberries (if in season); otherwise use frozen
- ½ C. fresh raspberries (if in season); otherwise use frozen
- 1 t. vanilla extract
- 1 t. artificial sweetener
- 4 C. ice

Directions:

Blend together all ingredients until the ice is crushed.

 This is great to drink while walking to class on those roasting summer days.

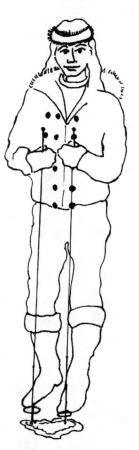

Would snow make a good slushy?

Notes:

Without Mom's Touch

When Mom Just Can't Be There

Feeling better Sweetie?

The Cure

When the "throne" seems too far away…you might want to try this cure, as explained to us by a little old Italian woman.

Ingredients:

  1 portion of white rice or Italian risotto

  1 whole lemon, cut into wedges

Directions:

Cook one portion of white rice/risotto according to the directions on the package. When cooked, fill one bowl with rice/risotto. Take the entire lemon, and cut it up into small wedges. Eat the entire lemon, skin and all, with the rice. Discard the seeds. It is amazing how well this works, most of the time…

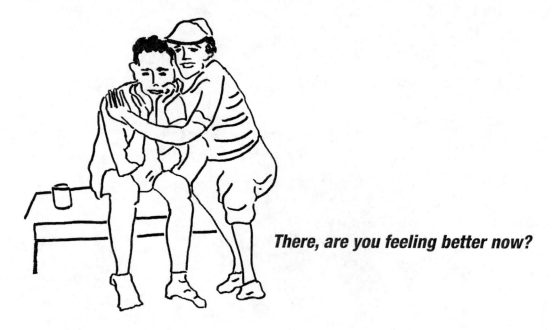

There, are you feeling better now?

Milk Toast

Ingredients:

- 1 piece white bread
- 1 t. butter
- 1 t. sugar
- 1 C. milk

Why get out of bed for milk toast?

Directions:

Toast one piece of bread. While it is toasting, heat one cup of milk to where it begins to steam, but do not boil. Place the toast in a bowl, add butter, and pour the hot milk over the toast. Sprinkle sugar on top.

Notes:

Chicken Noodle Soup and a Cozy Blanket

Ingredients:

1 whole chicken (Or this may be the time to
    buy a rotisserie chicken.)
1 C. onions, sliced
2 T. olive oil
1 C. celery
2 garlic cloves, minced
1 package egg-less noodles
½ t. celery seed
½ t. garlic salt
salt and pepper to taste

Directions:

Clean the chicken's cavity. Rinse, and place it in a large six-quart pot of salted boiling water. Cook for forty-five minutes or until chicken falls off the bone. Place chicken on a plate, and cool. Reserve cooking water. The water has now become your chicken stock. Bring six cups chicken stock to a boil, and lower the heat to a gentle rolling boil. Take the meat off the bones, and dice into cubes, set aside. Heat olive oil in a skillet. Cut the onion into thin strips, and sauté in the olive oil. When the onions are translucent, add the celery and garlic. When the celery is soft, put the onions, garlic, and celery into the pot of stock, and add the celery seeds. Add the package of egg-less noodles. Cook until noodles are done. Season with pepper, salt, and garlic salt to taste. Add the cubed chicken, and serve while hot.

This soup will stay fresh for several days in the refrigerator. When you don't want it anymore, that's when you'll know you're feeling better.

 Nobody cares how I feel.

Notes:

Creamy Broccoli Soup

My head is splitting.

Ingredients:

1 head broccoli

¼ C. butter

2 onions, sliced thin

1 garlic clove, crushed

2 C. celery, chopped

½ C. flour

4 C. milk

3 C. chicken broth

¼ t. marjoram

½ t. thyme

1 C. almonds, slivered

Directions:

Wash and cut broccoli into 1/2" slices. In a steamer basket, steam broccoli until slightly tender. In a large pan, melt butter, and sauté onions until tender. (They will look clear when they are done). Add the onions, celery, crushed garlic, and broccoli, and cook until tender. Gradually stir flour into the broccoli mixture. In the same pan, add milk slowly, while continuously stirring. Add chicken broth and herbs; stir until thickened. Salt and pepper to taste. Serve in bowls, and top with slivered almonds.

Cauliflower Soup with Sea Scallops

Ingredients:

6 T. olive oil, divided

1 C. celery, diced

2 C. sweet onion, diced

8 C. cauliflower, cut into florets

1 t. ground coriander

4 cans vegetable broth

15 sea scallops (frozen in fish section in your grocery store)

dash of cayenne pepper

1 can evaporated milk, fat free

salt and pepper to taste

Directions:

In a large pot, heat 4 T. oil over medium heat. Add the celery and onion, and sauté for five to six minutes, stirring occasionally. Stir in cauliflower and coriander. Add broth, and bring to a boil. Reduce heat to a gentle simmer for fifteen to twenty minutes. Remove from heat; let cool. Put soup mixture in a blender or food processor, and puree. Place back in the pot. Add milk, cayenne pepper, salt, and pepper. Heat over medium heat. Heat 2 T. of olive oil in a skillet. When oil is hot add scallops. They will stick to the pan when you first put them in the skillet. Let cook one minute. Shake the skillet to see if they are free. When they move, they are ready to flip. Flip and cook on the other side until they are free again. Then they are done. Cut the scallops in half, and drop in the soup.

I need my mom!

 Remember to wash your hands after handling the scallops.

Notes:

Tomato Soup and Peanut Butter Sandwich:

Sometimes you just have to open up a can!

Ingredients:

1 can low sodium tomato soup

1 can of water

2 slices of your favorite bread

peanut butter

jam

I just can't cook tonight.

Directions:

Put soup in small pot. Add water as directed, and heat. Make a peanut butter sandwich. Eat and go back to bed!

Its okay to use white bread when you're feeling sick, but when you're feeling better, switch back to whole wheat bread or five-grain bread. These breads not only taste delicious but add so much fiber and protein for your health.

Notes:

Mom's Vegetable Soup

Ingredients:

3 T. olive oil

1 C. onions, diced

1 C. carrots, diced

1 C. celery, diced

1 ½ C. unpeeled potatoes, cubed

1 C. canned corn

4 cans beef broth

3 C. low sodium tomato juice

1 C. frozen peas

2 cloves garlic, chopped

1 C. ketchup

salt and pepper to taste

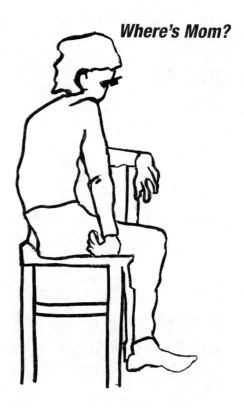

Where's Mom?

Directions:

Heat oil in a large pot. Sauté garlic. Add diced onions, and cook until they are translucent. Add carrots, corn, celery, and peas to the onions. Cook five minutes until slightly tender. Remember to stir as the vegetables are sautéing, so they don't burn. Add the broth, tomato juice, and ketchup, and bring to a gentle boil. Add remaining ingredients. Stir. Reduce heat to a simmer, and cook for approximately thirty-five minutes or until potatoes are tender.

Eat with a piece of warm bread, lying cozy in bed.

Dry Toast

Ingredients:

1 Piece of White bread

Directions:

Heat oven to 250 degrees. Put bread on flat tray and place on middle rack in the oven. Check every few minutes until bread is brittle and brown. The idea is to dry the bread, not to toast it.

Notes:

Banana Berry Good

Ingredients:

½ C. frozen blueberries

1 medium banana

1 C. fat free milk

½ t. vanilla

1 C. ice cubes

Directions:

Blend all ingredients together until the ice becomes crushed.

I feel so sad when I feel so bad...

Notes:

Fettuccine Comfort Food

Now that I'm here, you tell me you're feeling better?

Ingredients:

½ package fettuccine noodles

¾ C. half and half

4 T. butter, cut into pats

½ C. Parmesan cheese, grated

pinch of nutmeg

Directions:

Bring a large six-quart pot of water to a boil, and cook the fettuccine according to the package. Drain the fettuccine. Do not wash the pasta. In a large skillet, bring the half and half to a simmer. Do not boil. Cook for three minutes. Add the pasta to the half and half. Put in the pats of butter, and mix well while butter is melting. Add the Parmesan cheese and nutmeg. Mix all together and serve.

Notes:

Angel Hair Pasta with Chicken and Veggies

Ingredients:

1 store bought rotisserie chicken

3 T. olive oil, divided

1 garlic clove, minced

1 carrot, cut on the diagonal 1/4 thick

2 t. butter

1 C. broccoli florets

1 package angel hair pasta

Parmesan cheese (optional)

salt and pepper to taste

Directions:

Bring a large six-quart pot of water to a gentle boil, and cook the pasta according to the directions. Discard the skin on the rotisserie chicken, cut off the meat and set aside. In a large frying pan, heat 1 T. olive oil. When the oil is hot, put the garlic in. Cook until you can smell the garlic, but not until brown. Turn the heat down to medium, and add the carrots. Cook for two minutes, stirring the carrots so they don't burn. In the same pan, add the butter. When melted, add the broccoli florets, and cook an additional two minutes. Put the cut chicken in the pan, and cook until it is warm.

Drain the pasta in a colander. Do not rinse the pasta. Put in a large bowl, and toss with 2 T. olive oil. Put 2 C. of pasta in a bowl. Top with the vegetables and chicken. Salt and pepper to taste.

 Parmesan cheese is delicious sprinkled to top.

Feeling good!

Notes:

Index

Dessert

Dill

Dips

Drinks & Beverages

Staples

Tips and Substitutions

Tomato

Turkey